Understanding Cyberbullying
A Guide for Parents and Teachers

Professor Mona O'Moore is Fellow Emeritus of Trinity College Dublin and Adjunct Professor to the School of Education Studies at Dublin City University. She is also the Founding Director of the National Anti-Bullying Research and Resource Centre, formerly of Trinity College Dublin but now located within the School of Education Studies, Dublin City University. Former Professor and Head of School of Education in Trinity College Dublin, she is a graduate of Trinity College Dublin and gained an MA (Child and Educational Psychology) from University of Nottingham and a PhD (Psychology) from University of Edinburgh. She has written widely on the subject of bullying, with previous publications including *Dealing with Bullying in Schools: A Training Manual for Teachers, Parents and Other Professionals* (Sage Publications, 2004); *School Bullying: A Guide of Parents and Teachers* (Veritas, 2010), and *Bullying in Irish Education* (Cork University Press, 2013).

Mona O'Moore

Understanding Cyberbullying

A Guide for Parents and Teachers

VERITAS

Published 2014 by
Veritas Publications
7–8 Lower Abbey Street
Dublin 1, Ireland
publications@veritas.ie
www.veritas.ie

ISBN 978 1 84730 570 1

10 9 8 7 6 5 4 3 2 1

A catalogue record for this book is available from the British Library.

Designed by Heather Costello, Veritas Publications
Printed by Watermans Printers Ltd, Cork

Veritas books are printed on paper made from the wood pulp of managed forests. For every tree felled, at least one tree is planted, thereby renewing natural resources.

To my husband Rory and sons Garret, Olaf
and Runar for their encouragement and good
humour; to my brothers, Thor, Frode, Folke,
Bjørn and Geirr for their good company
throughout childhood and adulthood; and to all
those who touched me by sharing their individual
stories of victimisation.

ACKNOWLEDGEMENTS

This book would not have been possible without the generous assistance of school principals, teachers, parents and pupils who have contributed to my understanding of cyberbullying by their participation in research conducted by the Anti-Bullying Centre, formerly of Trinity College and now at Dublin City University. Also contributing to my understanding were individuals who took the time and courageously shared their very personal and touching stories of cyberbullying with me.

I wish also to express my gratitude to my husband, Professor Rory O'Moore, who, in spite of battling with the heavy burden of Alzheimer's disease, has kept me on my toes, selflessly reminding me that I had a book to write. He never ceased to draw my attention to any news item that made mention of cyberbullying, and hence this book has been able to draw on and make reference to important media reports on the subject. Having had red hair in his youth he can relate very well to bullying.

My sincere thanks also goes to my three sons, Garret, Olaf and Runar, who have all played their part in educating me about the wonders and dangers of the virtual world, thus preventing me from becoming stranded, for the time being at least, on the wrong side of the generational digital divide.

I am also grateful to Murray Smith, barrister at the Irish Bar and research assistant at the Anti-Bullying Centre (DCU), who kindly agreed to write the final chapter in the book on the legal implications of cyberbullying.

Finally, I wish to thank Donna Doherty of Veritas Publications for the confidence she has displayed in me by inviting me to write this book, and for her understanding and encouragement throughout.

CONTENTS

INTRODUCTION

Difficult as it has been to prevent and counter traditional bullying, cyberbullying poses significant new challenges for society. Our UN Secretary General, Ban Ki-moon, declared that homophobic bullying was a 'moral outrage, a grave violation of human rights and a public health crisis, it is also a loss for the entire human family when promising lives are cut short' (8 December 2011). The same can be said of cyberbullying as it too poses a serious threat to the health and well-being of children and teenagers.

While much cyberbullying among children and teenagers is activated outside of school hours, the hurtful behaviours and damage caused arise largely from relationship problems (e.g. intolerance, envy, break-ups and ganging up), which are formed during school hours. Thus, it is crucial that schools take leadership of this problem and develop policies and practices that will help all their members, namely the teachers, parents, pupils and the wider school community, to understand the problem and to take effective action.

In Ireland we are seeing an increasing growth of cyberbullying, with approximately one in four girls and one in six boys reporting that they have been targeted. Internationally, there is evidence which indicates that the more technogically advanced children become, the higher the rate of cyberbullying. As children of increasingly younger ages are owning and/or gaining access to mobile/smartphones and personal computers – the two main tools used to cyberbully – there is a clear risk of the problem growing. This means that younger and younger children, through no fault of their own, are at risk of being under attack from humiliating, threatening and sexually explicit messages and/or images. The perpetrators of cyberbullying also stand to lose as school bullying is a significant risk factor for a range of anti-social, criminal and health outcomes in later life. Evidence also points to the fact that across the world, the majority of children who are involved in cyberbullying are also involved in the traditional forms of bullying.

The most common methods that children and teenagers use to cyberbully one another are text messaging/images, emails, instant messaging, blogs, chat rooms and websites. Cyberbullying, like traditional bullying, is most often deliberate and persistent, but unlike traditional bullying it can more often be anonymous. It is this anonymity of cyberbullying that can be particularly unsettling and frightening for the victim. Adding salt to the proverbial wound is also the knowledge that any deeply disturbing messages and images that are sent or posted online are there for millions of people to see and potentially for an infinite period of time.

It is critical that children from as young an age as possible learn to refrain from cyberbullying. They must learn how to cope with it should they find themselves subjected to it or indeed be witness to it. It is also important that all who care for children and teenagers learn how they can best assist to prevent cyberbullying and to deal with it effectively.

While research in the field of cyberbullying is only emerging in comparison to the many studies on traditional bullying that have been carried out worldwide for over two decades, significant advances have been made. We have gained a good understanding of the nature of cyberbullying and the impact that it can have on those involved in it. Evidence is also available to indicate how cyberbullying can best be prevented and effectively dealt with once an assault has taken place.

Based on the most recent advances in the research of cyber-victimisation and cyber-perpetration, this book aims to give an understanding of cyberbullying – its prevalence, the characteristics of those involved in cyberbullying (i.e. the victims, bullies and bully-victims [one who both bullies and is a victim of bullying]), the impact of cyberbullying and the coping strategies commonly used by cyber-victims and their bystanders. It will also provide an understanding of how best cyberbullying can be identified, prevented and dealt with effectively by schools and especially by parents and teachers. Moreover, in the absence of specific legislation in Ireland that makes cyberbullying a criminal offence, this book offers an invaluable understanding of the existing laws in Ireland that can be applied to incidents of cyberbullying.

Throughout the book, I have included statements from children and teenagers to illustrate my viewpoints. It cannot be emphasised enough that to progress our understanding of a field that involves children as much as cyberbullying does, we need to listen to them. It is what they say that will enhance our understanding and guide us in developing the most effective policies and practices to tackle cyberbullying. It should also be noted that while I make reference throughout the book to children and teenagers who are involved in cyberbullying as 'cyber-victims', 'cyberbullies' and 'cyberbully-victims' I do not support the common practice of labelling children. The terms are used for convenience only. I strongly believe that with corrective action children and teenagers' behaviours can change – once a victim, bully or bully-victim not always a victim, bully or bully-victim.

Since my earlier book on school bullying,[1] we have seen a strong political will to tackle school bullying in all its forms. This has been marked by the *Action Plan on Bullying*,[2] launched in January 2013 by former minister for education, Ruairi Quinn, and Minister Francis Fitzgerald, formerly of the Department of Children and Youth Affairs. It was followed up, as promised, with the new *Anti-Bullying Procedures for Primary and Post-Primary Schools*.[3] It is hoped that the valuable and comprehensive understanding and the recommendations for best practice in these documents will, together with this book, motivate each reader to tackle cyberbullying. If each and every one of us as members of a school community or wider society take the required action that this book recommends as best practice, we will all contribute to preventing cyberbullying. We can also lessen the emotional burden of cyberbullying, one so heavy that it has cost the lives of some of our most treasured children and teenagers.

Notes

1. M. O'Moore, *Understanding School Bullying: A Guide for Parents and Teachers* (Dublin: Veritas, 2010).
2. Department of Education and Skills, *Action Plan on Bullying*, http://www.education.ie/en/Publications/Education-Reports/Action-Plan-On-Bullying-2013.pdf (2013).
3. Department of Education and Skills, *Anti-Bullying Procedures for Primary and Post-Primary Schools*, http://www.education.ie/en/Publications/Policy-Reports/Anti-Bullying-Procedures-for-Primary-and-Post-Primary-Schools.pdf (2013).

PART ONE

Understanding Cyberbullying

WHAT IS CYBERBULLYING?

Cyberbullying is often referred to as 'online bullying' and is also used interchangeably with the word 'cyber-harassment'. It is aggressive, wilful behaviour that is directed by an individual or group against another individual or group with the help of technological devices, primarily mobile/smartphones and the internet. It is a relatively new form of bullying, which has been growing fast since more and more people started to own mobile phones and have internet access. Cyberbullying is now a common part of bullying among children and teenagers.

Cyberbullying can consist of threats, insults, embarrassing or humiliating messages, pictures, video clips, defamation or impersonation. Insults can be identity- or prejudiced-based, expressing racist, sexist or anti-LGBT sentiments. However, it differs from face-to-face bullying, which is now often referred to as 'classical', 'traditional' or 'offline' bullying. With fewer boundaries or tangible consequences than with traditional bullying, children and teenagers are using technology to express their frustration, anger or indeed pleasure in ways that can be very destructive. This is illustrated by the following account of a schoolgirl from Dallas who was picked on because of her weight:

> She was called a 'fat cow MOO BITCH' on the school's message boards. Besides making fun of her weight, the anonymous writer also made fun of the fact that she suffered from multiple sclerosis, saying, 'I guess I'll have to wait until you kill yourself which I hope is not long from now, or I'll have to wait until your disease [MS] kills you.'[1]

In this case, the cyberbullying also became traditional bullying, with the student getting her car egged and a bottle of acid thrown at her front door, resulting in injury for her mother.

Due to the severe impact that cyberbullying has been found to have on the mental and physical health and education of those targeted there is considerable urgency to find effective strategies that will prevent cyberbullying and the associated anguish caused to victims.

In my book *Understanding School Bullying: A Guide for Parents and Teachers*, I described in some detail the different forms of traditional bullying, which can be both direct and indirect, and can take the form of verbal attacks, physical aggression or assaults, gestures, exclusion or extortion.[2] There is general agreement among researchers that traditional bullying has three main criteria:

- Intention to cause harm to the victim
- Repetition of the abusive behaviour over a period of time
- An imbalance of power between the victim and bully/bullies.

While traditional bullying can be psychological and indirect (such as spreading rumours with the perpetrator unknown to the victim), cyberbullying is exclusively psychological and affords the perpetrator much greater opportunity to remain anonymous.

Defining Cyberbullying

To date, it is to be noted that there is no universal agreement as to how cyberbullying should be defined. This is undoubtedly why the research literature varies between and even within countries with regard to the extent of cyberbullying and the characteristics associated with those involved in cyberbullying. Without agreement on what exactly we mean by 'cyberbullying', reliable and valid measures of its frequency will not be possible. However, there is strong agreement among researchers that cyberbullying, like traditional bullying, is deliberate and that there is an imbalance of power. Yet there is less agreement over whether a cyber-attack needs to be repeated in order to be defined as cyberbullying.

While there is agreement that cyber-attacks have to be intentional in order for them to be defined as cyberbullying, disagreement may arise depending on whether one takes the perpetrator or the victim's perspective. Most often, intentionality and impact are interchangeable. For the victim the weight is commonly placed on the impact rather than the intent of the cyber-attacks.

The balance of power may be less obvious in relation to cyberbullying than with traditional bullying. In respect of traditional bullying it tends to refer to physical attributes (such as strength, height and weight) or psycho-social attributes (such as intelligence, popularity and socio-economic status). With cyberbullying the same features can apply, in particular if the victims know the bully's identity (for example, that they are physically stronger, smarter and have an aggressive personality). However, if the bully is anonymous, power in the cyber world can take the form of technological skills and the anonymity of the sender as well as the victims' powerlessness to control the time and physical location of the cyber-acts.

There is no safe haven for victims of cyberbullying. The only way they can protect themselves from attacks is by not answering or logging on to their phones or computers. However, as the internet is increasingly the lifeline to their peers and even to their studies, this would prove intolerable for most children and teenagers.

The main reason cyberbullying is different to traditional bullying is that it need not be repeated – a single cyber-act has the potential to be seen instantly by multiple viewers and over an indefinite period of time, which constitutes repetition for the victim. Each attack has the potential to gain a permanent status in cyberspace, and whether the comments or images posted are deliberately malicious or just careless, they can be a source of repeated hurt to the victim. For example, Snapchat, a messaging application that allows sent photos to be viewed by the recipient for a maximum of ten seconds before they disappear, can be screengrabbed and subsequently shared (although the sender is alerted when a screengrab of their message is taken). By the time an offensive message or image is removed from a public forum (social-networking sites, blogs and video-sharing websites such as YouTube), it may have already been saved and shared by others. Thus, all indirect electronic communications should be considered as having a potentially permanent digital record.

However, a single act of cyber-aggression should not be judged as cyberbullying when the communication (for example text, photo, video clip or email) is sent directly to the person it is intended to hurt. In such cases it should be deemed as a one-off act of cyber-aggression, equivalent to a written letter marked 'personal and confidential'. But as with traditional bullying, if the direct communication carries a severe threat, which serves the purpose of intimidating the recipient on an prolonged basis, then, in my opinion, it would be reasonable to deem even a one-off act as constituting cyberbullying.

Making the distinction between direct and indirect acts of cyber-aggression is supported by the Department of Education and Skills' new *Anti-Bullying Procedures for Primary and Post-Primary Schools*. They point out, for example, that a single cyber-attack constitutes cyberbullying when the cyber-message or image is intentional and placed on a public forum for multiple viewers to see for an indefinite period of time, causing the victim repeated distress. However, 'isolated or one-off incidents of intentional negative behaviour, including a one-off offensive or hurtful text message or other private messaging, do not fall within the definition of bullying and should be dealt with, as appropriate, in accordance with the school's code of behaviour'.[3]

Using the above as a guide, it would seem prudent for the purpose of policies and sanctions to define 'cyberbullying' as any cyber-aggression that is activated:

- with the intent to cause harm
- when there is an imbalance of power
- when the act constitutes repetition.

What Makes Cyberbullying Different from Traditional Bullying?

We have already seen that a major difference between cyber and traditional bullying is that cyberbullying can more often be defined, although not exclusively, on the basis of one-off aggressive acts.

Other differences are:

- Cyberbullying allows the aggressor to have access to the victim anytime and anywhere. With no safe haven the bullying can be relentless.
- Cyberbullying has the potential to reach a much wider audience than traditional bullying, undoubtedly adding to the victim's humiliation and despair.

- Cyberbullying, in contrast to traditional bullying, is more invisible to the adult eye; cyberspace allows for much greater freedom from adult supervision.
- Cyberbullying allows greater opportunities for anonymity and false identities than traditional bullying. This reduces the aggressors' fear of being held accountable and also adds to the anxiety and mistrust of the victim.
- Cyberbullying provides the sender with no facial/emotional reactions to an attack.
- Cyberbullying allows perpetrators to reach their victims from anywhere on the planet. In the absence of any European or international anti-bullying legislation, cyberbullying that takes place across countries does not lend itself readily to prosecution.
- The attributes that make for the imbalance of power for cyberbullying (e.g. technological skills) differ from that of traditional bullying (e.g. physical strength).
- Cyberbullying provides greater opportunity for inter-generational bullying than would be possible in the 'real' world; for example, teacher are at a greater risk of being cyberbullied by their students.

Cyberbullying Acts

When considering cyberbullying acts, it is common to distinguish between the method used to share the abusive behaviour – email, text, etc. – and the form that behaviour takes, such as flaming (hostile and profane online interaction) or lewd texts. Keith Sullivan describes a five-step programme in carrying out an act of cyberbullying (steps 2, 3 and 4 do not need to be activated in that order):

1. The decision is taken to initiate a cyber-attack
2. The technology is chosen (mobile/smartphone, computer, tablet, gaming console)
3. The cyberbullying tactic is chosen (flaming, outing, impersonation, etc.)
4. The method is chosen to place and display the hostile cyber behaviour (emails, texts, chat rooms, photos, video clips)
5. The decision to launch or not to launch the planned attack is made.[4]

Cyberbullying Tactics

Most books and websites that deal with cyberbullying have included cyberbullying tactics. With the growth of the internet, as well as children's adeptness in handling digital technology, it is to be expected that these tactics will change as the technology changes. Michael Nuccitelli, a forensic psychologist and one of the authors of iPredator, a cyberbullying education and information website, has provided what is possibly the most comprehensive list of cyberbullying tactics currently in use, tactics that are likely to be with us into the future. I have included them here with minor adaptions and a few exceptions:

1. **Exclusion:** Social exclusion occurs by indirectly sending a hurtful message to the victim to let them know that they are not welcome to participate in social activities. This is highly effective because it directly targets a child's need to feel accepted and to belong to a group.

2. **Flaming:** Creating passionate online arguments that frequently include profane and vulgar language. The online arguments occur in public forums (e.g. discussion boards, groups and chat rooms) for peer bystanders to witness. The intent is to assert power and to establish a position of dominance over a victim.

3. **Exposure:** Includes the public display, posting or forwarding of personal communication, images or videos by the cyberbully to the victim. The impact is exacerbated when the very personal material is sexual in nature.

4. **Intimidation:** This is used to instil fear in the victim by communicating threats, which can sometimes be physical, via emails that not only inform the victim but also others.

5. **Cyber-harassment:** Sending hurtful messages to the victim that are worded in a severe, persistent or pervasive manner. The content is always negative and frequent.

6. **Phishing:** Tricking, persuading or manipulating the victim into revealing personal and/or financial information about themselves and/or their loved ones. The information is then used to purchase items in the name of the victim or the victim's parents.

7. **Impersonation:** Impersonating or 'imping' involves impersonating the victim so that comments sent to peers, including friends on social networking sites, forums, message boards and chat rooms, appear

as if they have come from the victim. The cyberbully can also set up websites to tamper with the victim's profile, thus damaging the victim's reputation or friendships.

8. Denigration or 'dissing': Sending, posting or publishing cruel rumours, gossip and untrue statements about the victim with the intent to damage their reputation or friendships. The purpose is to humiliate and belittle the victim.

9. Mobile device image sharing: Sending images directly to peers who can then send them to everyone in their address books. Some will post these images on video sites, their social networking profiles and other programmes for anyone to download or view. If the images are pornographic this form of information exchange can become a criminal act.

10. Non-consensual image and video dissemination: Images and videos of the victim are emailed to peers, while others are published on video sites like YouTube with the view to humiliate and embarrass the victim.

11. Interactive-gaming harassment: Online gaming devices allow children to interact with each other. This enables the cyberbully to verbally abuse the victim, lock them out of the game and pass on false information to others. Cyberbullies can also hack into the victim's account. Children may be unaware that they are targeted until fellow players alert them to it.

12. Pornography and marketing-list insertion: Signing the victim up to pornography and/or junk marketing emailing and instant messages from pornography sites and advertising companies. This naturally can be a cause of great embarrassment and frustration and can lead to victims being falsely accused as the source for these lists or websites and unfairly punished.

13. Cyberstalking: Includes threats of harm, intimidation and/or offensive comments sent through information and communication channels, giving the victim the feeling that the threats are real and could become real offline stalking. Cyber-stalking is regarded as the most dangerous cyberbullying tactic and one that requires immediate adult attention.

14. Griefing: This involves manipulating the playing experience of players in a multiplayer online game. The motivation of the cyberbully is less to do with winning the game and more to do with ruining the playing experience of the others. Behaviours typically include bad language, blocking certain areas of the game and cheating.

15. Password theft and lockout: The cyberbully steals the victim's password and chats to others, impersonating the victim. Once they are confident the peers believe it is the victim they become provocative and argumentative, causing the victim's friends or strangers offence and anger. The cyberbully also locks the victim out by changing their password. Not having access to their username or email account, the victim is unable to close or show that they are not the offensive, confrontational person.

16. Webpage assassination: The cyberbully creates, designs and posts websites that insult the victim and also their peers or groups of people who may share similar characteristics, such as the victim's race, religion or sexual orientation.

17. Voting and polling booth degradation: The cyberbully makes use of websites that offer polling/voting features free of charge and creates webpages that allows others to vote on the victim's physicality or personality, such as 'ugliest', 'fattest', 'dumbest', etc.

18. Bash boards: These are online bulletin boards which allow the cyberbully to post critical, hateful and belittling information about the victim for all to read and to share with others.

19. Trickery (hoodwinking): Similar to phishing, the cyberbully purposely tricks the victim into divulging secrets, private information and embarrassing information about themselves, then publishes the information online. The victim is tricked by thinking the sensitive material will be presented by the cyberbully in a positive light.

20. Happy slapping: This involves the cyberbully taking pictures or videos of the victim being physically assaulted and then posting the images online for public consumption in order to cause the victim maximum hurt and embarrassment.

21. Text wars and attacks: The cyberbully and a group of accomplices gang up on the victim by sending hundreds of emails or text messages. Quite apart from the emotional toll it takes on the victim, it can also cause parental rebuke due to escalating mobile phone charges.

22. Malicious code dissemination: This tactic allows cyberbullies to send viruses, spyware and hacking programmes to a victim, which can be very costly to repair. As children become more adept in Information and Communication Technology (ICT) it is expected that this tactic will become more frequent.

23. Warning wars: This involves making false allegations to an internet service provider that the victim is posting inappropriate or abusive information. By doing this repeatedly the victim may have their account suspended, and if the cyberbully has also informed the parents of the victim it may cause the victim an additional telling off until the matter is cleared up.

24. Screen-name mirroring: The cyberbully uses screen names and user names almost identical to the victim's own name to send messages, meaning that those receiving the information may not be spotting the minor differences and think it was sent by the victim.

25. Cyber drama: A passive-aggressive tactic which involves gossip that is not supposed to be shared on a blog, or a 'flame war' that ends after a few messages.

26. Lewd texts/Sexting: This refers to text messages or images of a sexually explicit nature which are created to embarrass the victim when distributed and shared with others online.

27. Pseudonym stealth: The cyberbully develops a nickname unknown to the victim in order to keep their identity secret as they proceed to taunt, tease and humiliate the victim.

28. Instant messaging attacks: This is a very popular form of communication to harass, taunt and threaten the victim when online in a chat room situation. The conflicts that arise online can also often extend to face-to-face bullying.

29. Cyberbullying by proxy: This is the term used when the cyberbully encourages or manipulates others to become accomplices in harassing the victim. It is especially dangerous as adults may become accomplices to the cyberbully, not knowing the victim is a child.

30. Social media cyberbullying: The cyberbully persuades the victim to include them on 'friends' lists. The bully then unashamedly proceeds to spread malicious information about the victim.

31. Digital piracy inclusion: This tactic entices the victim to engage in illegal reproduction and distribution of copyrighted material on the internet and then the cyberbully reports the victim to relevant authorities for digital piracy, which has legal and criminal implications.

32. Slut-shaming: This targets primarily females and occurs when the cyberbully publishes sexually provocative images or videos of the victim obtained without her consent.

33. Trolling: This involves baiting the victim to encourage and provoke conflict, as well as sending insulting messages intended to inflame emotions of others so that a 'flame war' is created in public places, such as chat rooms or social-networking sites.

34. Sextortion: This disturbing tactic involves the cyberbully extorting images of sexual behaviour from the victim in exchange for not making sensitive material public. For example, a story came to light recently which involved young girls being secretly filmed in various stages of undress in their bedrooms by a computer hacker who had commandeered their webcams using malware. The cyberbully blackmailed his victims to provide even more images, videos and online chat sessions. If they refused, he threatened to post the images online in order to humiliate them.[5]

35. Twitter pooping: This involves using Twitter to ridicule and humiliate the victim. With the hostile communication restricted to 140 characters, 'net lingo' is increasingly used to convey the insults.

36. Micro-visual cyberbullying: This involves using Viddy, which shares bite-sized videos restricted to fifteen seconds, or Snapchat to send menacing messages.

To these cyberbullying tactics I would add:

Grooming: A predatory practice through which children and teens fall victim to adults who develop relationships without revealing their true identities in order to gain sexual favours. This is often carried out using webcams, but could lead to in-person meetings to commit acts of sexual abuse. Recently, a man aged thirty-six had sex with a number of girls after posing as a teenage boy online.[6]

Cyberbullying Methods

It is clear that there is no shortage of ways in which perpetrators can get at their intended victim. With the help of smartphones, desktop computers, laptops, tablets and gaming consoles, the common methods of cyberbulling are:

1. **Mobile phone call:** This is a popular means to communicate verbally and, as with landlines, is a source of silent or persistent abusive calls. Phone numbers can be blocked to hide the identity of the caller. Cyberbullies can also steal the victim's phone and use it to harass others, causing the victims to be blamed.

2. **Text messaging (SMS):** Texting is one of the most common methods of cyberbullying among Irish teenagers, with girls favouring it to boys. Unfortunately, pay-as-you-go handsets make it difficult to trace the perpetrators, therefore hiding the bully's identity.

3. **Picture/video clips:** This method is favoured by boys. Very clear images can be captured and uploaded online or via Bluetooth and shared with others, with the potential of causing immeasurable distress. Now that photos can be easily doctored, there is considerable potential to depict the victim in a very undesirable light.

4. **Email:** This method allows cyberbullies to abuse victims directly, or by way of setting up multiple accounts or adopting a pseudonym to reduce the risk of being caught. Sending anonymous emails from an internet café also makes identification of the perpetrator difficult, as the Internet Protocol (IP) address will only lead one to the café.

5. **Chat rooms:** Together with chat rooms on game sites, consoles and virtual worlds, the social and fun environment provided by chat rooms has the potential to become a forum for negative behaviours.

6. **Social-networking sites:** Almost one-third of seven- to eleven-year-olds have their own Facebook profile, despite the fact the minimum age specified for membership is thirteen.[7] Without due attention paid to security settings, social-networking sites are frequently used to spread false and hurtful rumours so as to damage the reputation of the account holder. Children and teenagers who feel under pressure to have many 'friends' are especially at risk of being targeted.

7. **Websites:** Four out of ten Irish teenagers access their favourite website every day, and two-thirds do so at least three times a week.[8] The skills required to create websites to good effect can also be misused by cyberbullies to defame their victims by publishing nasty information directly onto the victim's profile or by setting up a fake profile pretending to be the victim. They can also hack the victim's real profile and change their personal information.

The cyber-behaviours and methods used to persecute victims as outlined above, while by no means exhaustive, indicate the need for parents and teachers to keep abreast of the manner and means by which children can be targeted by their peers and strangers. In the latter parts of this book we will look at the strategies that can be used by schools, teachers and parents to help prevent and counter the current growth of cyberbullying which, as will be made clear in Chapter 5, can have devastating effects on the victim.

Chapter 1: Key Messages

- Cyberbullying is a new form of bullying, which has arisen due to the spread of technology.
- Cyberbullying involves sending or posting hurtful, humiliating or threatening text or images with the help of phones, the internet or other electronic devices.
- Other forms of cyberbullying include creating embarrassing and offensive websites, polling classmates about the victim's physical attributes and popularity, and excluding victims from online and gaming groups.
- Unlike traditional bullying, there is no safe haven for victims of cyberbullying, who can be reached in their homes at any time of day or night.
- Short of keeping phones and computers switched off, it is difficult to avoid being distressed by the material sent or posted.
- Children accessing the internet and social-networking sites are getting increasingly younger, thus putting themselves at risk of being victimised.
- The growth of cyberbullying requires parents, teachers and school management to work together on prevention and intervention strategies.

Notes

1. S. Keith and M. E. Martin, 'Cyberbullying: Creating a Culture of Respect in a Cyber World', *Reclaiming Children and Youth* 13 (2005): pp. 224–8.
2. M. O'Moore, *Understanding School Bullying: A Guide for Parents and Teachers* (Dublin: Veritas, 2010).

3. Department of Education and Skills, *Anti-Bullying Procedures for Primary and Post-Primary Schools* (2013): p. 40. http://www.education.ie/en/Publications/Policy-Reports/Anti-Bullying-Procedures-for-Primary-and-Post-Primary-Schools.pdf (accessed 1 September 2014).
4. K. Sullivan, 'Action Against Cyberbullying (AAC): A Programme for Understanding and Effectively Addressing School-Related Cyberbullying', *Bullying in Irish Education: Perspectives in Research and Practice*, M. O'Moore and P. Stevens, eds (Cork: Cork University Press, 2013), pp. 291–319.
5. J. Mooney, 'Sextortionist Forced Irish Teen to Strip', *Sunday Times* (29 September 2013).
6. R. Mc Cullen, '"Predator" (36) Had Sex with Girls After Posing as Teenage Boy on Site', *Irish Independent* (16 November 2013).
7. D. Holloway, L. Green and S. Livingstone, *Zero to Eight: Young Children and Their Internet Use* (London: LSE, 2013).
8. *Get With It!: A Parents' Guide to Social Networking Websites* (Dublin: Office for Internet Safety, 2011).

THE PREVALENCE OF CYBERBULLYING IN IRELAND

A recent EU Kids Online study, the largest and most representative study to date, found a wide variation in the prevalence of cyberbullying across Europe among children aged nine to sixteen.[1] Online victimisation ranged from 2% to 14%. Being the target of nasty or hurtful messages was the most common form of online bullying. Having the hurtful messages passed around the peer group or posted for others was less common.

Of the Irish children who participated in the survey, it was found that 4% were bullied online, and 4% were bullied via mobile phones calls, texts or image/video texts. Social-networking sites constituted the main platform for online forms of bullying. Instant messaging was confined to teenagers only, whereas gaming websites provided a bullying platform for children aged eleven and older.

It was found that 11% of our eleven- to sixteen-year-olds reported having seen or received sexual messages online. This number increased sharply as the respondents' age increased, from 3% of eleven- and twelve-year-olds to 21% of fifteen- and sixteen-year-olds.

When traditional bullying was examined, the authors of the report[2] found that in contrast to the 4% of children and teens who admitted to being cyberbullied, there were 15% who reported that they were bullied face to face, meaning traditional bullying is just over three times more common than cyberbullying.

Unfortunately, no comparable numbers are available from the EU study for children who cyberbullied others. Our own study on cyberbullying, which was conducted three years earlier than the EU study and comprised 3,004 twelve- to seventeen-year-olds (1,009 girls and 1,995 boys), found that 8.5% of the Irish teenagers surveyed had cyberbullied others.[3] Almost one in five (18.3%) admitted to being involved in cyberbullying either as victim, bully or bully-victim. Of these, the incidence rate for each of the status groups were as follows:

- 9.8% cyber-victims (6.9% boys; 15.6% girls);
- 4.4% cyberbullies (3.5% girls; 4.9% boys);
- 4.1% cyberbully-victims (4.5% girls; 3.9% boys).

Studies in Northern Ireland show incidence rates that are not dissimilar to our Irish study.[4] For example, a study of eleven- to fifteen-year-olds showed that 19.3% of respondents admitted to being involved in cyberbullying:

- 11.9% were cyber-victims;
- 3.1% were cyberbullies;
- 4.3% were cyberbully-victims.

Other worldwide studies have also displayed similar findings to those in Ireland.[5] However, studies of cyberbullying from Canada and the United States of America have reported exceptionally high rates of cyberbullying.[6] Whenever comparisons are made of prevalence rates of bullying, whether traditional or cyber, it has to be borne in mind that differences found may be due to a combination of the following factors:

- The measurements used: for example, was it based on self-reports, teacher or peer reports?
- The definition: was there one? If so, what criteria were used to define bullying?
- The age of the respondents
- The options the children were given when asked to respond: some studies just ask for a 'yes' or 'no', while others ask children to discern whether they were bullied 'once or twice', 'sometimes', 'once a week or daily', etc.
- The typology used: was a distinction made between those who were bullied only (pure victims) and those who cyberbullied only (pure bullies) and those who both bullied and were bullied (bully-victims)?
- The cut-off points for the classification of bullies and victims: some studies, for example, have excluded children who answer they have bullied 'once or twice' as not being involved in bullying.

Even though the levels of cyberbullying in Ireland are among the lowest recorded worldwide, there can be no room for complacency. If we take the very conservative prevalence rate of 4% as recorded in the EU Kids Online study of Irish nine- to sixteen-year-olds, this means that there are 40,000 school children in the country experiencing cyberbullying. As access to technology and cyberbullying are related, every effort needs to be made to avoid an escalation of the problem.[7]

Overlap Between Cyber and Traditional Bullying

The majority of children and adolescents involved in cyberbullying have also been found to be involved in traditional bullying. For example, in our study of cyberbullying of twelve- to sixteen-year-olds, the majority (71%) of the cyber-victims were also victims of traditional bullying, while over one-quarter (28.9%) were also traditional bullies. Of those who admitted to cyberbullying others, over two-thirds (67.4%) reported that they also engaged in traditional bullying. Almost one-third of the cyberbullies (32%) reported that they were also victims of traditional bullying.[8]

Early researchers into cyberbullying saw the overlap between cyber and traditional bullying as signalling that, for traditional victims in particular, the internet may be a place to assert dominance over others as compensation for being bullied in person. Children not involved in conventional bullying spoke of how the internet provides them with a place 'where they take on a persona that is more aggressive than their in-person personality'. In addition, the researchers Ybarra and Mitchell argued that the asymmetrical power that distinguishes cyberbullying from traditional bullying gives cyberbullying the edge on asserting dominance. They found that the majority of cyber-aggressors knew their victims, whereas the aggressor was unknown to most victims.[9]

Gender and Cyberbullying

Some international studies have found no significant gender disparity in cyberbullying experiences,[10] whereas others have found girls to be more involved in cyberbullying than boys.[11] In our Irish study we found that there were almost three times as many girls than boys who were cyber-victims.[12] While more boys admitted to being cyberbullies, the difference between girls and boys was very small. Indeed, girls have been known to under-report the extent to which they conventionally bully, in which case this may also be true of their cyberbully status in our study. However, there is little doubt that cyberbullying affords girls the opportunity to use indirect and non-physical forms of bullying. Female bullying is associated with covert and verbal tactics, often while seeking entertainment, revenge born of envy or jealousy, or when competing for social status among peers.[13]

A Finnish study has shown that the most common profile was to be victimised by same-sex peers only; while the second most common was bullying by both same-sex and opposite-sex peers. To be bullied by the opposite sex alone or in combination with other types of perpetrators (e.g. unknown adults and unknown persons of unknown age and sex) was significantly more common among girls.[14]

In our Irish study, girls were found to be the primary targets for the majority of the cyber-abuse methods. However, where boys have been found in the international literature to be more often the victims of a particular method of cyberbullying, the methods have differed from one study to the next. In our study, for example, boys more than girls were subjected to bullying by photo and video clips.[15]

Boys in our Irish study perpetrated all forms of cyberbullying somewhat more than girls, with the exception of bullying in online chat rooms. Their preferred method was via photos or video clips, whereas girls preferred texting, which finds support in a more recent Irish study of teenage girls cyberbullying.[16]

Age and Cyberbullying

As is the case with traditional bullying, age-related variations have been found to characterise cyberbullying. However, whereas traditional bullying tends to be more common among pre-teens, a sharp increase with age has been found in respect of cyberbullying throughout Europe, with older teens becoming involved. This is perhaps not surprising in view of the relationship between cyberbullying and access to electronic devices, and possibly the decline in supervision and monitoring of older teens.

With regard to the Irish participants in the EU Kids Online study, 1% of nine- to ten-year-olds had been bullied online. This rose to

9% for the fifteen to sixteen age group. Similarly, 1% of nine- to ten-year-olds, in contrast to 10% of fifteen- to sixteen-year-olds, admitted to experiencing hurtful or nasty behaviour via mobile phone calls, texts or images/videos.[17] However, age difference often depends on the method being used to cyberbully. For example, our study found that text messaging, picture bullying, abusive mobile calls and instant messaging were more common among our first-, second- and third-year students than among the older fourth-year students. It was encouraging, however, to note that while there was a steady increase in almost all the forms of cyberbullying up until third year of post-primary school, there was a significant decrease during fourth year.[18]

Whether the decline reflects increased maturity or contextual factors is uncertain. It is possible that the change from the exam-focused Junior Cycle to the less exam-oriented Transition Year programme makes for a more relaxed and co-operative learning environment, which dissipates the boredom, jealousies and power struggles that are often triggered in a competitive environment. It is also possible that as children grow older they come to better appreciate the need for moral standards in cyberspace.

Young Children and Their Internet Use

The number of young people who use electronic communication has not only steadily risen over the years, but those accessing the internet have become increasingly younger. For example, a 2010 study by the Department of Health and NUI Galway found that 29.8% of girls and 20.8% of boys aged ten to eleven communicated with their friends by phone, text or email daily. This rose to 59.5% for girls aged twelve to fourteen and 42.8% for boys of the same age. By age fifteen to seventeen, 72.3% of girls and 53.3% of boys were using electronic communication with friends every day.[19] More recently, it was reported that there are many children under nine online.[20] In South Korea, the country with the world's highest high-speed internet penetration, 93% of three- to nine-year-olds go online for an average of eight to nine hours a week. No figures are available for Ireland, but closer to home in the UK, one-third of three- to four-year-olds go online using a desktop PC, laptop or netbook, 6% use a tablet computer and 3% use a mobile phone. In addition, 87% of five- to seven-year-olds in the UK go online.[21] The introduction of touch-screen devices will undoubtedly see these rates increase among toddlers and preschool children, as well as young school children. As young children may not have the critical skills needed to keep safe when they interact and play in virtual worlds, parents and teachers are required to be vigilant to prevent the risks of cyberbullying.

Chapter 2: Key Messages
- Cyberbullying affects a substantial number of our school-going population.
- A considerable proportion of cyberbullies are also traditional bullies. Some are even traditional victims.
- A high incidence of cyber-victims are traditional victims. A significant number of cyber-victims are also traditional bullies.
- One-third of teens have been witness to cyberbullying.
- Any child who is in possession of a mobile phone or computer can be a cyberbully or a cyber-victim.
- Girls are more likely to be cyberbullied and boys to cyberbully. However, the literature is not unequivocal in relation to gender and cyberbullying.
- Irish victims reported phone calls and texting as the most common forms of cyberbullying.
- Irish cyberbullies, especially boys, favour using photos and video clips as a means of cyberbullying.
- Educational endeavours are necessary to promote respect and consideration when using electronic forms of communication.
- Children accessing the internet are becoming increasingly younger, which requires adults to become more vigilant of the risks of cyberbullying.

Notes
1. S. Livingstone, L. Haddon, A. Görzig and K. Ólafson, *Risks and Safety on the Internet: The Perspective of European Children* (London: LSE, 2011).
2. B. O'Neill, S. Grehan and K. Ólafson, *Risks and Safety for Children on the Internet: The Ireland Report* (London: LSE, 2011).
3. M. O'Moore, 'Cyberbullying: The Situation in Ireland', *Pastoral Care in Education* 30 (2012): pp. 209–23.

4. C. McGuckin, 'Bullying in Schools in Northern Ireland', *Bullying in Irish Education: Perspectives in Research and Practice*, M. O'Moore and P. Stevens, eds (Cork: Cork University Press, 2012).

5. H. Gleeson, *The Prevalence and Impact of Bullying linked to Social Media on the Mental Health and Suicidal Behaviour Among Young People: A Review of the Literature* (2014), www.education.ie (accessed 1 September 2014).

6. B. Holfeld and M. Grabe, 'An Examination of the History, Prevalence, Characteristics and Reporting of Cyberbullying in the United States', *Cyberbullying in the Global Playground*, Li, Cross and Smith, eds (London: Wiley-Blackwell, 2012).

7. Holfeld and Grabe (2012), op. cit.

8. O'Moore (2012), op. cit.

9. M. L. Ybarra and K. J. Mitchell, 'Online Aggressors/Targets, Aggressors, and Targets: A Comparison of Associated Youth Characteristics', *Journal of Child Psychology and Psychiatry* 45 (2004): pp. 1308–16.

10. Livingstone, Haddon, Görzig and Ólafson (2011), op. cit.

11. Li, Cross and Smith (2012), op. cit.

12. O'Moore (2012), op. cit.

13. J. E. Field, J. B. Kolbert, L. M. Crothers and T. M. Hughes, *Understanding Girl Bullying and What to Do About It* (London: SAGE, 2009).

14. A. Sourander, A. B. Klomek, M. Ikonen, J. Lindroos, T. Luntamo, M. Kosklainen, T. Ristkari and H. Helenius, 'Psychosocial Risk Factors Associated With Cyberbullying Among Adolescents', *Arch Gen Psychiatry* 67 (2010): pp. 720–8.

15. R. M. Kowalski, S. P. Limber and P. W. Agatston, *Cyberbullying: Bullying in the Digital Age* (London: Wiley-Blackwell, 2012).

16. D. Ging and J. O'Higgins Norman, 'Teenage Girls' Understanding of Cyberbullying in an Irish Second-Level School', *Gender and Education* (forthcoming, 2014).

17. O'Neill, Grehan and Ólafson (2011), op. cit.

18. M. O'Moore and S. J. Minton, 'Cyberbullying: The Irish Experience', *Handbook of Aggressive Behaviour Research*, C. Quin and S. Tawse, eds (Hauppage, NY: Nova Science Publishers, 2009), pp. 269–92.

19. Department of Health and National University of Ireland, Galway, *Health Behaviour in School-aged Children* (2010), Research Factsheet, 20.

20. D. Holloway, L. Green and S. Livingstone, *Zero to Eight: Young Children and Their Internet Use* (London: LSE, 2013). Also available at www.eukidsonline.net.

21. Ibid.

3

WHO ARE THE VICTIMS OF CYBERBULLYING?

There is general agreement among researchers that the more frequent a child or teen's use of the internet, the greater the risk is that they will become a victim of cyberbullying.[1] It is not surprising, therefore, that parental mediation has been shown to play a critical role in reducing cyber-victimisation. Parental mediation is defined as 'the activities which are carried out by parents to protect their children from exposure to online dangers'.[2] 'Evaluative mediation' involves discussions with the child or teenager about internet safety and creating rules regarding online activities together, with the placement of the family computer in a public place. 'Restrictive mediation', on the other hand, involves activities such as limiting the amount of time that a child or adolescent spends online, or using filtering software to limit which sites a child is allowed to visit. Where parents establish rules for internet use and place computers in public places, as well as having filtering software on the computers, victimisation was found to be reduced. Yet this level of monitoring could cause some tension and studies have shown that when children have a poor relationship with their parents, more cyber-risks are encountered.[3]

Cyberbullying victims have been found to share many characteristics with children who are bullied using more traditional methods.[4] This is perhaps to be expected in view of the considerable overlap of cyber with traditional bullying highlighted in Chapter 2. Having reviewed the literature on cyberbullying, Helen Gleeson also shares the view that one of the consistent predictors of being a cyber-victim is being a victim of traditional bullying. She states that victims of traditional relational and social bullying (such as those who are excluded from peer groups and have rumours spread about them in order to undermine their social relationships) are also highly likely to be cyber-victimised.[5]

In *Understanding School Bullying: A Guide for Parents and Teachers*, I stressed that anyone can become a victim of traditional bullying by being in the wrong place at the wrong time. However, most at risk were those children and teenagers who had:

- An anxious, sensitive, shy, insecure and cautious temperament
- Fewer good friends
- Low self-esteem
- A passive, non-aggressive or non-assertive manner
- An emotionally reactive manner
- A clumsy entry behaviour when trying to join a peer group.[6]

There is evidence to show that most of the social and emotional characteristics listed above can also be applied to children and adolescents subjected to cyberbullying.[7] For example, our Irish study showed that cyber-victims shared not only low self-esteem with traditional victims, but also a higher level of neuroticism and greater feelings of anxiety. However, in contrast to traditional victims they did not perceive themselves to be more unpopular.[8]

While the number of friends is not synonymous with popularity, especially in cyberspace where youngsters will boast of having hundreds of 'friends' on Facebook, having a social group has not been found to protect children from cyberbullying in the way it does from traditional bullying. Indeed, this finding prompted the authors of one study to remark that cyberbullying was perhaps not simply 'a new wine in an old bottle'.[9]

The same study, which comprised 7,508 adolescents in the United States as part of the collaborative World Health Organisation cross-national study, noted that adolescents from the higher socio-economic classes were at greater risk of cyber-victimisation. However, the authors pointed out that this was likely to have been due 'to the greater availability of computers and cell phones for adolescents from wealthier families'.[10]

Regarding scholastic achievements, victims of cyberbullying – like their traditional counterparts – often have higher achievement levels than their perpetrators.[11] Being a so-called 'swot' or 'nerd' has always put children at risk of being targeted. However, the findings in relation to academic achievement and cyber-victimisation have not been as consistent as with traditional bullying.[12]

Exploring the psychological make-up of cyber-victims further, and examining in particular self-esteem, social stress, depressive symptoms, locus of control and self-efficacy has added support to

40

our Irish findings. Essentially, both cyber and traditional forms of victimisation are associated with lower self-esteem and self-efficacy, as well as higher stress, anxiety, depressive symptoms and locus of control. Even controlling for traditional forms of bullying have shown cyberbullying to be a significant predictor for all the above outcome measures.[13] The relationship between depressive symptoms and cyberbullying, in particular, finds much support from studies worldwide. In the same way, my own research has shown that the frequency of traditional bullying impacted adversely on self-esteem.[14] There is substantial evidence to suggest that as the frequency of cyber-victimisation increases, so too do depressive symptoms.[15]

A study that looked specifically at cyber-victimisation and its relationship to loneliness and depressive mood examined both components of loneliness, social and emotional. The emotional facet includes feelings of loneliness resulting from a lack of intimate friends, whereas the social facet encapsulates 'the distress feelings of loneliness experienced as a result of the lack of a wider social network when young people feel that they do not belong to any community, or that they do not have friends or allies that they can rely on'.[16] In measuring depressive mood, the participants were asked to rate themselves on statements such as 'No one really loves me', 'All the bad things are my fault' and 'I am sad all the time'. The researchers found that the adolescents who were cyber-victims expressed a higher sense of loneliness, both social and emotional, and a stronger depressive mood than those who were not cyber-victims. They explained the findings in one of two ways. The first is that young people with a more intense sense of loneliness and depressive mood may have difficulties in developing social networks. Because of limited social experiences they may seek more social connections online and as a result may become more vulnerable to being targeted. The second argument is that 'low peer acceptance may be an indication of limited social skills, resulting in the lack of friends, which then adversely affects and intensifies their sense of loneliness'.[17]

It is noteworthy that lonely children have been found to communicate personal and intimate topics significantly more often online than those who do not report that they are lonely. For example, they communicate 'how they feel, serious problems, things that bother them, secret or confidential things, their health, things they would not say to someone's face, gossip/rumours, things in the past, things they have done that day, and they ask someone to be their friend'.[18] They also communicate with adults online. These behaviours alone are contra-indicative of safe online behaviour and as such would increase the risk of being targeted by cyberbullies.

The same study also revealed that victims of major chat room victimisation exhibited socially manipulative behaviour more frequently, such as false statements concerning their age or sex, or the spreading of lies. The researchers argued that such behaviour may serve as a protective purpose, helping victims to avoid further bullying and making them less vulnerable to victimisation through the creation of a false identity. It is however also conceivable, as they state, that chat room victims develop a 'false chat identity' as a disguise in order to discuss their real personal weaknesses and problems with other chatters.[19] This in turn could signal to other chat room visitors that they are an easy target and provoke victimisation.

Another significant finding was that the chat room victims were more likely to be chat room bullies than traditional school bullies, namely, they demonstrated bullying behaviour exclusively in the environment of their victimisation.[20] This finding, of course, may suggest that these victims belong to the group of bully-victims identified in the research on traditional bullying.

While there is strong support to indicate that lonely children and adolescents value the internet as a communicative 'protected' environment in which 'they can better express their inner selves and find conversations more satisfying than they do offline',[21] as a result of a lack of longitudinal studies, it is not possible to say with any degree of certainty whether the social and emotional characteristics attributed to cyber-victims preceded the victimisation or emerged as a result of being bullied. Future studies would benefit from tracking the direction of socio-emotional characteristics – such as social anxiety, loneliness and depression – to further examine the timing of these effects as children progress from childhood through to adolescence. Hopefully in time, *Growing Up in Ireland*, a national longitudinal study of children, will be able to fill some of the gaps in our current knowledge regarding the psychological make-up of cyber-victims.[22]

However, the relationships noted so far between psycho-social characteristics and cyber-victimisation, whether due to cause or effect, have implications for the prevention and intervention of cyberbullying. For example, social skills training and practice in internet safety is a must. Parents and teachers need to become more involved in their children's internet activities. Taking into account the relationship between loneliness and depressive mood, it will be necessary to focus on developing adolescents' ability to establish intimate relationships and to develop social integration in order to diminish vulnerability to cyberbullying.[23]

Chapter 3: Key Messages

- Cyber-victims share many of the characteristics of traditional victims.
- The characteristics which have been found to distinguish cyber-victims from non-victims are low self-esteem, reduced well-being, social anxiety, loneliness and depressive mood.
- Cyber-victims spend more time online and disclose more personal information than non-victims.
- Participation in social networks increases the risk of becoming a cyber-victim.
- The protective value of friends that characterises traditional bullying does not benefit cyber-victims.
- Cyber-victims' parents may keep less of a watchful eye on their online activities than those of non-victims.
- Intervention and prevention programmes need to focus on internet safety skills.
- Parents need to become more aware of their children's online activities, whether they be phone or computer based.
- Social skills training and social integration will contribute to preventing and tackling cyberbullying.

Notes

1. H. Gleeson, *The Prevalence and Impact of Bullying linked to Social Media on the Mental Health and Suicidal Behaviour Among Young People: A Review of the Literature* (2014), www.education.ie (accessed 1 September 2014).
2. G. S. Mesch, 'Parental Mediation, Online Activities, and Cyberbullying', *Cyberpsychology and Behaviour* 12 (2009): pp. 387–93.

3.   S. Livingstone and J. E. Helsper, 'Taking Risks When Communicating on the Internet: The Role of Offline Social–Psychological Factors in Young People's Vulnerability to Online Risks', *Information, Communication and Society* 10 (2007): pp. 619–44.

4.   C. Katzer, D. Fetchenhauer and F. Belschak, 'Cyberbullying: Who Are the Victims? A Comparison of Victimisation in Internet Chat Rooms and Victimisation in School', *Journal of Media Psychology* 21 (2009): pp. 25–36.

5.   Gleeson (2014), op. cit.

6.   M. O'Moore, *Understanding School Bullying: A Guide for Parents and Teachers* (Dublin: Veritas, 2010).

7.   R. M. Kowalski, S. P. Limber and P. W. Agatston, *Cyberbullying: Bullying in the Digital Age* (London: Wiley-Blackwell, 2012).

8.   L. Corcoran, I. Connolly and M. O'Moore, 'Cyberbullying in Irish Schools: An Investigation of Personality and Self-Concept', *The Irish Journal of Psychology* 33 (2012): pp. 153–65.

9.   J. Wang, R. J. Iannotti and T. R. Nansel, 'School Bullying Among Adolescents in the United States: Physical, Verbal, Relational, and Cyber', *Journal of Adolescent Health* 45 (2009): pp. 368–75.

10. Ibid.

11. Q. Li, 'Cyberbullying in Schools: A Research of Gender Differences', *School Psychology International* 27 (2006): pp. 157–70.

12. D. Cross, H. Monks, M. Hall, T. Shaw, Y. Pintabona, E. Erceg, G. Hamilton et al., 'Three Year Results of the Friendly Schools Whole-of-School Intervention on Children's Bullying Behaviour', *British Educational Research Journal* 37 (2011): pp. 105–29.

13. B. K. Fredstrom, R. E. Adam and R. Gilman, 'Electronic and School Based Victimisation: Unique Contexts for Adjustment Difficulties During Adolescence', *Journal of Youth and Adolescence* 40 (2011): pp. 405–15.

14. M. O'Moore and C. Kirkham, 'Self-Esteem and Its Relationship to Bullying Behaviour', *Aggressive Behaviour* 27.2 (2001): pp. 69–83.

15. S. Perren, J. Dooley, T. Shaw and D. Cross, 'Bullying in School and Cyberspace: Associations with Depressive Symptoms in Swiss and Australian Adolescents', *Child and Adolescent Psychiatry and Mental Health* 4.28 (2010): pp. 1–10; J. Wang, T. R. Nansel and R. J. Iannotti, 'Cyberbullying and Traditional Bullying: Differential Association with Depression', *The Journal of Adolescent Health: Official Publication of the Society for Adolescent Medicine* 48.4 (2011): pp. 415–17.

16. D. Olenik-Shemesh, T. Heiman and S. Eden, 'Cyberbullying Victimisation in Adolescence: Relationships with Loneliness and Depressive Mood', *Emotional and Behavioural Difficulties* 17 (2012): pp. 361–74.

17. Ibid.

18. Katzer, Fetchenhauer and Belschak (2009), op. cit.

19. Ibid.

20. Ibid.

21. L. Bonetti, M. A. Campbell and J. Gilmore, 'The Relationship of Loneliness and Social Anxiety with Children's and Adolescents' Online Communication', *Cyberpsychology, Behaviour and Social Networking* 13 (2010): pp. 279–85.

22. www.growingup.ie.

23. L. Bonetti (2010), op. cit.

4

WHO ARE THE CYBERBULLIES?

As with cyber-victims, research is limited regarding the specific characteristics of those children and teenagers who become cyberbullies. However, given that traditional bullies are more likely to engage in cyberbullying[1] it is to be expected that although there may be distinct features, traditional and cyberbullies will have many features in common.

The characteristics of traditional bullies include the following:

- A strong need to dominate, to feel powerful and to be in control
- Easily frustrated and angered
- A positive attitude to aggression
- A tough poise showing little empathy
- Do not readily take responsibility for their behaviour, blaming the victim instead
- Both proactive (deliberate and calculating) and reactive (defensive response to provocation) in their aggressive behaviour.[2]

Of all the risk factors associated with traditional bullying, it is of note that a longitudinal study of boys has shown that the most significant risk factors are high hyperactivity-impulsiveness and low empathy.[3] While the latter study did not distinguish between those who bullied only (pure bullies) and those who were both bullies and bullied (bully-victims), there is general agreement that bully-victims, while fewer in number to pure bullies, are more troubled.[4]

They have been characterised as having:

- An emotional reactive manner, e.g. a tendency to fly off the handle at the slightest provocation
- Social skills deficits, e.g. clumsy behaviour when attempting to join a peer group
- Negative attitudes and beliefs about themselves and others.

Importantly, children who bully by any method are not born but made, meaning that in addition to the above behavioural characteristics there are causal factors at play – home, school, community and societal. Factors found to contribute to traditional bullying in the home, for example, are:

- A lack of warmth and involvement
- Permissiveness of aggression
- Physical punishment and violent emotional outbursts
- Negativism on the part of the mother
- Negativism between the parents.

Worryingly, a summary report of parenting styles and discipline in Ireland shows a heavy reliance on power-assertive methods of child-rearing. For example, almost half of all parents (47.6%) admitted to shouting or swearing at their child and a quarter reported having used physical punishment, with higher levels for children in the younger age groups.[5]

Schools also have been found to contribute to and in some cases exacerbate the level of aggression in pupils. The factors that have been found to be most responsible are:

- Inconsistent and inflexible rules
- Poor staff morale
- Inadequate supervision
- Punishment that is too harsh, abusive or humiliating
- Few incentives for rewards for non-aggressive behaviour
- A curriculum that affords too few feelings of success and achievement.

Research is not sufficiently advanced to give a definitive profile of a child or adolescent who engages in cyberbullying. A factor that has complicated our understanding to date is the lack of consensus around the definition of 'cyberbullying' (as discussed in Chapter 1). Not all researchers, therefore, have distinguished between cyberbullying and one-off acts of cyber-aggression or between pure cyberbullies and cyberbully-victims. It is likely, therefore, that the psychological profile for children who repeatedly harass a peer by sending or posting nasty messages or images for all to see (i.e. cyberbullying) will be different from that of children who have sent one angry message for the sole attention of the target (cyber-aggression).

With these limitations in mind, traits that have been found to characterise children and adolescents who cyberbully are as follows:

- Impulsive
- Aggressive
- Dominant
- Difficulty adhering to rules
- Susceptible to changing moods
- Manipulative
- Low empathy (both affective and cognitive)
- Displacement and diffusion of moral responsibility (moral disengagement)
- Low self-esteem
- Socially anxious
- Have been bullied first.[6]

Although low empathy has been consistently associated with traditional bullying, it has been argued that cyberbullies may experience less empathy for their victims than even traditional bullies. The reasons given are that either the anonymity or distance between the cyberbully and the victim prevents the cyberbully from observing the immediate consequences of their behaviour, or that cyberbullying may attract persons with low-trait empathy.[7]

Coupled with low empathy in cyberbullies is a lack of moral standards and moral affect.[8] However, the high level of moral disengagement or lack of remorse found in traditional bullies has not been found to the same extent in cyberbullies; although one study found age was a factor, with cyberbullies aged thirteen to fifteen demonstrating higher levels than the sixteen- to eighteen-year-olds.[9] If age differences in moral disengagement can be replicated in future studies then it is to be expected that they have a bearing on age trends in cyberbullying. There is already some evidence that the greatest incidence is around thirteen to fifteen years, and decreases after late adolescence.[10]

As is the case with adults, there are many children and teenagers who write things online that they would never say in person. This phenomenon of feeling removed from their own actions and their intended victim is known as the 'disinhibition effect',[11] as is well demonstrated by this quote:

> With the internet, you can get away with a lot more because I don't think a lot of people would have enough confidence to walk up to someone and be like, 'I hate you, you're ugly'. But over the internet you don't really see their face or they don't see yours and you don't have to look in their eyes and see they're hurt.[12]

The disinhibition effect may go some way to explaining why adolescents perceived as more powerful or threatening in real life have been found more likely to be targets of cyber-aggression than traditional aggression[13] and why 'half of youth who admitted to cyberbullying said they did so because they had been bullied first'.[14]

The scope for anonymity on the internet also allows children and adolescents to take on new ways of behaving in a manner not dissimilar to hiding behind a mask at a fancy dress party. This concept is commonly referred to as 'deindividuation' and was developed to explain the phenomenon that people in crowds act in ways that might not normally be endorsed.[15] In other words, the anonymity afforded by the internet allows a child and teenager to be guided by social norms other than their own personal code of morality.

However, a well-designed and highly regarded study involving 2,215 Finnish adolescents (aged thirteen to sixteen) found pure cyberbullies to have a high level of perceived difficulties.[16] They felt unsafe at school and uncared for by their teachers. They also had a high number of headaches. In addition, they shared the following attributes with their traditional counterparts:

- A high level of conduct problems
- Hyperactivity
- Frequent smoking and drinking
- Low pro-social behaviour.

Moreover, a study of 2,017 Greek adolescents showed that impulsive use of the internet was predictive of adolescents victimising others online.[17] While the literature has been divisive in relation to the self-esteem of traditional bullies,[18] there is strong evidence to suggest that cyberbullies lack self-esteem.[19]

Insomnia has been found also to be elevated in the cyberbully group.[20] While I am not aware of any studies focusing on online behaviour at night time, it would be worthwhile to examine whether it is during periods of insomnia that adolescents may activate cyberbullying attacks. As with victims, the more time children and adolescents spend online, the higher the risk that they will engage in cyberbullying.[21] Furthermore, risky internet usage (such as disclosing private information and sharing passwords) has also been found to be a significant predictor of involvement in cyberbullying.[22]

In reviewing the risk factors associated with cyberbullying behaviour it is important to recognise that while pure cyberbullies share many of the characteristics of traditional bullies, they have been found to be less aggressive. Irish research, for example, showed that not only did the pure cyberbullies not display the high psychoticism levels of pure traditional bullies, but they did not suffer from the insecurities that the traditional bullies displayed across the domains of self-esteem.[23]

However, when children engage in both traditional and cyberbullying there is an escalation of anti-social behaviour. Lower levels of effortful control, higher rates of manipulativeness, remorselessness and reactive and proactive aggression have been reported, which suggests that cyberspace and other technological advances merely provide additional mediums through which aggressive youth can act.[24] Furthermore, the students who are most likely to become involved in cyber-aggression are those who are most likely to be identified by teachers, peers or parents as already aggressive in offline situations. The combined bullies (traditional and cyber) have also been found to show the highest levels of reactive and instrumental (pre-meditated/calculating) aggression compared to traditional bullies, cyberbullies and non-bullies.[25]

Cyberbully-victims
Like traditional bully-victims, children and adolescents who are involved in cyberbullying in the roles of both bully and victim have

49

been found to be the most troubled and most at risk of adjustment problems. They share all the psychiatric and psychosocial risk factors of both bullies and victims.[26]

Bully-victims have also the highest levels of reactive and instrumental aggression compared to their traditional counterparts and adolescents who are not involved in bullying.[27] As noted in Chapter 2, girls are more at risk of being involved in cyberbullying as both victim and bully, and this may explain why cyber-bullying related suicides in Ireland (as far as can be judged by media reports) mostly involve girls.

Motives for Cyberbullying

Important as is an understanding of the characteristics of children and adolescents who cyberbully, it is also necessary to understand their motives for initiating the many different forms of attack discussed in Chapter 2. As motives differ among those who cyberbully, solutions will need to take account of these motivations.

The reasons and triggers for cyberbullying which were put forward and expanded on by European partners are as follows:

- Bullying being seen as normal
- Boredom
- Intercultural conflicts between children of different nationalities
- Tensions and conflicts in the classroom
- Friendship break-ups or change
- Personal information (details, photos/videos) not intended for the public being passed on – sometimes even with no malicious intent.[28]

However, a study of eleven- to fourteen-year-olds examined four underlying motives of bullying, looking at both traditional and cyberbullying.[29] The motives were:

- to show that I am more powerful (power)
- to be accepted by my friends (affiliation)
- because it was fun (fun)
- because I was angry (anger).

The findings showed that children who exclusively cyberbullied were motivated mainly by anger and less so by fun. The motives for affiliation and power were low. For the 'traditional bullies' the main motive was also anger but the other three motives were rarely mentioned. For the combined bullies (cyber and traditional) anger was again the main motive. Although they were also motivated by power, affiliation and fun, these motives were not as dominant as anger. Gender differences showed boys to be more motivated by power and fun than girls.

Other motives identified as being involved in cyberbullying are revenge, boredom, meanness, attention, looking cool and tough, jealousy and the pleasure of inflicting pain.[30] Undoubtedly added to this list are bigotry and prejudice. In an Irish study, most online conflicts between girls arose from jealousies over boys. Strategies of exclusion were used, such as posting comments or pictures about sleepover parties on Facebook, knowing that someone who wasn't invited would see them.[31]

An oft-used classification of the motives for cyberbullying comes from an expert in cyberlaw, Parry Aftab, who has made a distinction between the 'vengeful angel', 'the power-hungry', 'mean girls' and the 'inadvertent cyberbully' (or 'because I can').[32]

The *vengeful angel* does not see him or herself as a bully. They see themselves as 'Robin Hoods of cyberspace', righting wrongs or protecting themselves from the person who caused them upset. They are not a victim of cyberbullying but may be a victim of traditional bullying and their motivation is to protect others in cyberspace. Thus, this type of cyberbully often gets involved trying to protect a friend who is being bullied either online or offline. However, they tend to work alone and anonymously to avoid being physically attacked by the traditional bully they are trying to neutralise. An example of the vengeful angel is the student in our Irish study who, when asked what he did when he witnesses someone being bullied, responded, 'I turn the bully into a victim'.[33] It has been noted that in some instances, the vengeful angel will engage in cyberbullying not only out of anger but also envy and jealousy.[34]

The *power-hungry* cyberbully resembles the proactive traditional bully who is intent on exerting control, power and authority. Unlike the vengeful angel, they enjoy an audience to witness or reinforce their actions. They are essentially 'looking for attention and want to see their target(s) sweat'.[35] Their preferred cyberbullying tactic is a direct attack or threat sent to their victims or communicated in a game, hacking attacks, or public posting. If they do not get a reaction they may escalate their activities, substituting insults for threats.

Aftab is of the opinion that there is a subgroup of power-hungry cyberbullies who seek power as a means of compensating for their own perceived inadequacies. These children may be victims of traditional bullying and may be female or physically smaller than many of their peers. Cyberbullying provides a means to retaliate. Family and friends of this subgroup tend not to be aware that they are bullying others as they tend to work anonymously, not sharing their actions with others, and even cyberbully by proxy. Because of this and their tech skills, Aftab is of the opinion that they can be the most dangerous of all cyberbullies.

The *mean girls* type of cyberbullying is not restricted to girls, but usually occurs when children or adolescents are bored and looking for entertainment. This form of bullying is typically done in groups and requires an audience. It may occur in the school library, canteen or at a sleepover. They want others to know who they are and to show they have the power to cyberbully others. To be effective they must get others to help by actively passing along emails or instant messages filled with rumours, poll voting at the cyber-bashing sites, or by doing something that will help to spread the humiliation and make their victims a source of ridicule. These bully groups can grow with peer support and lack of positive bystander intervention. On the other hand, when no entertainment value is forthcoming it tends to die out.

The *inadvertant cyberbully* does not think of themselves as a bully. Rather, they wish to put on a tough persona online or they are acting in response to a hateful or provocative message that they have received. In responding, they tend not to think about the consequences of their actions before clicking 'send'. They are, therefore, surprised when they are accused of cyberbullying. This type of cyberbully can also be someone who is roleplaying, acting out their aggressive fantasies online. It may be a child who is well behaved, polite and a good student in real life. However, they behave differently online, simply because they can. Indeed, 13% of European children reported that they had pretended to be a different kind of person online.[36]

The findings and observations presented above all have implications for prevention and intervention of cyberbullying that will be addressed in Parts 2 and 3 of the book in relation to what schools, their staff and parents can do to tackle the problem.

Chapter 4: Key Messages

- Bullying is learned behaviour, with the behaviour and normative beliefs of peer group, home, school and society contributing to the development of aggressive attitudes and behaviour.
- Cyberbullies spend more time accessing and engaging in risky online behaviour.
- Cyberbullies share physical, psychological and academic traits with their traditional counterparts.
- Compared to non-bullies, cyberbullies are more aggressive (reactive and proactive), hyperactive, impulsive, anti-social and have conduct problems, low empathy and low self-esteem. Smoking and alcohol are also heavily used and headaches and insomnia are elevated.
- Cyberbullies are predominantly motivated by anger and to a lesser extent by power, fun and affiliation. Other motives have also been found to play a part, such as revenge, jealousy and boredom.
- Cyberbully-victims are the most troubled, sharing the psychosocial difficulties of cyberbullies and cyber-victims.

Notes

1. F. Sticca, S. Ruggieri, F. Alsaker and S. Perren, 'Longitudinal Risk Factors for Cyberbullying', *Journal of Community & Applied Social Psychology*, 23 (2012): pp. 52–67.
2. M. O'Moore, *Understanding School Bullying: A Guide for Parents and Teachers* (Dublin: Veritas, 2010).
3. D. P. Farrington and A. C. Baldry, 'Individual Risk Factors for School Bullying', *Journal of Aggression, Conflict and Peace Research* 2 (2010): pp. 4–16.
4. A. Sourander, A. B. Klomek, M. Ikonen, J. Lindroos, T. Luntamo, M. Kosklainen, T. Ristkari and H. Helenius, 'Psychosocial Risk Factors Associated With Cyberbullying Among Adolescents', *Arch Gen Psychiatry*, 67 (2010): pp. 720–8.
5. Office of the Department of Children and Youth Affairs, *Parenting Styles and Discipline: Parents and Children's Perspectives: Summary Report*, The National Children's Strategy Research Series (2010).

6. P. R. Ang and H. D. Goh, 'Cyberbullying Among Adolescents: The Role of Affective and Cognitive Empathy and Gender', *Child Psychiatry and Human Development* 41 (2010): pp. 387–97; J. Patchin and S. Hinduja, 'Cyberbullying and Self-Esteem', *Journal of School Health* 80 (2010): pp. 614–21; R. M. Kowalski, S. P. Limber and P. W. Agatston, *Cyberbullying: Bullying in the Digital Age* (London: Wiley-Blackwell, 2012); G. D. Floros, E. Konstantinos, V. Fisoun, E. Dafouli and D. Gerouklis, 'Adolescent Online Cyberbullying in Greece: The Impact of Parental Online Security Practices, Bonding, and Online Impulsiveness', *Journal of School Health* 83 (2013): pp. 445–53; A. Almeida, I. Correia, S. Marinho and G. D'Jamila, 'Virtual But Not Less Real: A Study of Cyberbullying and its Relations to Moral Disengagement and Empathy', *Cyberbullying in the Global Playground: Research from International Perspectives*, Li, Cross and Smith, eds (London: Wiley-Blackwell, 2012).
7. G. Steffgen, A. Konig, J. Pfetsch and A. Melzer, 'Are Cyberbullies Less Empathic?: Adolescents' Cyberbullying Behavior and Empathic Responsiveness', *Cyberpsychology, Behaviour, and Social Networking* 14 (2011): pp. 643–8.
8. S. Perren and E. Gutzwiller-Helfenfinger, 'Cyberbullying and Traditional Bullying in Adolescence: Differential Roles of Moral Disengagement, Moral Emotions and Moral Values', *European Journal of Developmental Psychology* 9 (2012): pp. 195–209.
9. Almeida, Correia, Marinho and D'Jamila (2012), op. cit.
10. P. K. Smith, G. Steffgen and R. Sittichai, 'The Nature of Cyberbullying and an International Network', *Cyberbullying Through the New Media: Findings From an International Network*, P. K. Smith and G. Steffgen, eds (London: Psychology Press, 2013).
11. J. Suler, 'The Online Disinhibition Effect', *Cyberpsychology and Behaviour* 7.3 (2004): pp. 321–26.
12. Media Smarts, Canada's Centre for Digital and Media Literacy, Cyberbullying Backgrounder, http:// mediasmarts.ca/backgrounder/cyberbullying-backgrounder (accessed 19 January 2014).
13. L. M. Sontag, K. H. Clemens, J. A. Graber and S. T. Lyndon, 'Traditional and Cyber Aggressors and Victims: A Comparison of Psychosocial Characteristics', *J. Youth Adolescence* 40 (2011): pp. 392–404.
14. Media Smarts, Canada's Centre for Digital and Media Literacy, 'Who Cyberbullies and Why', http://mediasmarts.ca/backgrounder/cyberbullying/who-cyberbullies-and-why (accessed 10 January 2014).
15. E. Diener, 'Deindividuation: The Absence of Self-Awareness and Self-Regulation in Group Members', *The Psychology of Group Influences*, P. B. Paulus, ed. (Hillsdale, NJ: Lawrence Erlbaum Associates, 1989): pp. 209–42.
16. A. Sourander, A. B. Klomek, M. Ikonen, J. Lindroos, T. Luntamo, M. Kosklainen, T. Ristkari and H. Helenius, 'Psychosocial Risk Factors Associated With Cyberbullying Among Adolescents', *Arch Gen Psychiatry* 67 (2010): pp. 720–8.
17. G. Floros, K. E. Siomos, V. Fisoun, E. Dafouli and D. Geroulakis, 'Adolescent Online Cyberbullying in Greece: The Impact of Parental Online Security Practices, Bonding, and Online Impulsiveness', *Journal of School Health* 83 (2013): pp. 445–53.
18. M. O'Moore and C. Kirkham, 'Self-Esteem and Its Relationship to Bullying Behaviour', *Aggressive Behaviour* 27 (2001): pp. 269–83.
19. J. Patchin and S. Hinduja, 'Cyberbullying and Self-Esteem', *Journal of School Health* 80 (2010): pp. 614–21.

20. V. Kubiszewski, R. Fontaine, K. Hure and E. Rusch, 'Cyberbullying in Adolescents: Associated Psychosocial Problems and Comparison with School Bullying', *Encephale* 39 (2013): pp. 77–84.

21. F. Sticca, S. Ruggieri, F. Alsaker and S. Perren, 'Longitudinal Risk Factors for Cyberbullying in Adolescence', *Journal of Community and Applied Social Psychology* 23.1 (2012): pp. 52–67.

22. O. Erdur-Baker, 'Cyberbullying and its Correlation to Traditional Bullying, Gender and Frequent and Risky Usage of Internet-Mediated Communication Tools', *New Media and Society* 21.1 (2010): pp. 109–25.

23. L. Corcoran, I. Connolly and M. O'Moore, 'Cyberbullying in Irish Schools: An Investigation of Personality and Self-Concept', *The Irish Journal of Psychology* 33 (2012): pp. 153–65.

24. Sontag, Clemens, Graber and Lyndon (2011), op. cit.

25. P. Gradinger, D. Strohmeier and C. Spiel, 'Motives for Bullying Others in Cyberspace: A Study on Bullies and Bully-Victims in Austria', *Cyberbullying in the Global Playground: Research from International Perspectives*, Li, Cross and Smith, eds (London: Wiley-Blackwell, 2012).

26. Sourander, Klomek, Ikonen, Lindroos, Luntamo, Kosklainen, Ristkari and Helenius (2010), op. cit.

27. Gradinger, Strohmeier and Spiel (2012), op. cit.

28. M. O'Moore, O. Samnoen, C. McGuckin, N. Crowley, L. Corcoran and R. H. Rasmussen, 'How Parents Can Detect, Intervene and Prevent Cyberbullying', *CyberTraining4Parents*, www.cybertraining4parents.org.

29. Gradinger, Strohmeier and Spiel (2012), op. cit.

30. Kowalski, Limber and Agatston (2012), op. cit.

31. D. Ging and J. O'Higgins Norman, 'Teenage Girls' Understanding of Cyberbullying in an Irish Second-Level School', *Gender and Education* (forthcoming, 2014).

32. P. Aftab, 'Stop Cyberbullying', www.wiredsafety.net (2011) (accessed 13 April 2014).

33. M. O'Moore, 'Cyberbullying: The Situation in Ireland', *Pastoral Care in Education* 30 (2012): pp. 209–23.

34. Kowalski, Limber and Agatston (2012), op. cit.

35. Aftab (2011), op. cit.

36. S. Livingstone, L. Haddon, A. Görzig and K. Ólafson, *Risks and Safety on the Internet: The Perspective of European Children* (London: LSE, 2011).

THE EFFECTS OF CYBERBULLYING

Children and adolescents crave close peer relationships, and in adolescence social status and peer relations take on greater importance. To be accepted by peers, including those of the opposite sex, is of vital importance in the development of an adolescent's identity. To be denied intimacy and belonging can give rise to feelings of loneliness, and if accompanied by a sense of negative mood this may develop into depression. To be bullied threatens children's need for friendship and belonging, not to mention the need for competence and to be in control of one's future. How children and teenagers interpret and respond to threats to their social and emotional needs will determine the impact of the victimisation.

We have known for some time now that traditional victimisation can result in social and emotional difficulties, low self-esteem, scholastic underachievement, school absenteeism and dropping out, substance abuse, anxiety, loneliness, depression, psychosomatic symptoms, sleep disturbances, self-harm, suicidal ideation and suicide.[1] And while research examining the effects of cyberbullying is still in the early stages, there is growing evidence that the negative outcomes of cyber-victimisation can range from 'trivial levels of distress and frustration to serious psychosocial and life problems'.[2] The outcome depends on the frequency, length and severity of the malicious acts. There is also some evidence to suggest that ill-effects are magnified the younger the victims are.[3] It is also to be expected that social or emotional vulnerabilities that precede cyber-victimisation will be felt more strongly.

When cyberbullying continues over a period of time there is a high risk that it will damage the victim's physical and emotional well-being, leading to a lowering of self-esteem and depression,[4] with higher levels of depressive symptoms in cyber-victims than in traditional victims.[5]

Nor are one-off incidents to be underestimated. These can also have severe effects, as was the case with the pictures taken of a teenage girl performing a sex act at a concert that took place at Slane Castle in 2013. The photographs spread online with frightening speed: 'Hundreds shared the photos as many alternatively mocked the girl, or praised her sexual partner as a hero.' Although social media companies tried to block access to the images, it was too late 'to contain an ever-expanding number of retweets, shares and likes'.[6] It was reported that the victim was hospitalised as result of the cyberbullying.[7]

It is argued that it is the victim's perception of the pervasiveness of the message or image that will influence the impact.[8] Recognising that any message or image can be damaging in its own right, it is likely that the impact will be even greater when there is reputational damage and the knowledge that an infinite number of individuals will see the potentially damaging content, providing opportunities for new, unknown perpetrators to continue the victimisation.

The tragic deaths by suicide of Irish teens reported in the last year are a testimony to the destructive power of cyberbullying among young people.[9] When the identity of the cyberbully is not known to the victim the psychological impact can become even greater, increasing the sense of powerlessness and fear. Other emotions which have been found to follow episodes of cyberbullying are:

- A change in habits in the use of phone or computer, from obsessive checking to avoiding the technology or being secretive, nervous or on edge when accessing it
- Frustration and high levels of anger
- Emotional distress, sadness and tearfulness
- Feeling unsafe
- Social anxiety, panic attacks
- Shame, embarrassment and self-blame, which often prevents victims from reporting their victimisation and seeking help
- Disillusionment and distrust of peers
- Loneliness, due to the absence of companionship and the lack of a wider social network
- Lack of confidence and depreciated levels of self-esteem.[10]

Specific examples from Irish teenagers interviewed included:

> 'It had me crying and it made me feel like nobody is my friend.'
> 'It made me feel horrible, as if I was a waste of space and nobody cared.'
> 'I feel upset, I don't know who to trust. Is it my friends spreading rumours or is it my fault?'
> 'I feel worthless, suicidal.'[11]

As with traditional bullying, being cyberbullied can affect concentration and scholastic achievements.[12] The preoccupation with their cyberbullying experiences translates itself to a sudden drop in the victim's grades.[13] Feeling that they can no longer function well or feel safe in school, victims may skip classes and miss valuable school days, possibly resulting in detentions and suspensions. There are also reports that a significant number of cyber-victims feel that their home life has significantly suffered from being cyberbullied.[14] Most worrying is the finding that cyber-victims are eight times more likely than other young people to take a weapon to school.[15]

While victims of traditional bullying can find sanctuary in their own homes, cyberbullying leaves victims with no escape unless they cease to use their phones or computers. It is not surprising, therefore, that the hurtful, offensive or threatening messages, photographs or video clips can reach and wear down their targets. As one victim remarked, 'It would make me feel scared and threatened, I'd be embarrassed – scared in my own home.'[16] Furthermore, to be cyberbullied by an adult of the same or opposite sex, a stranger or a group of people has been found to create a significant fear in the victim for their own safety, indicating possible trauma.[17]

That depression and suicide ideation can so easily manifest themselves is hardly surprising in light of the range of emotions associated with cyber-victimisation – loneliness, helplessness, embarrassment, upset, anger and fear, to list the most common.[18] As exposure to childhood trauma has been linked to psychotic experiences such as hearing voices,[19] parents and professionals need to become alert to the tell-tale signs of cyberbullying and work together to find effective means to prevent it. However, in committing to preventing cyberbullying, we must not lose sight of traditional bullying. It is when cyberbullying is combined with traditional bullying that the risk of suicide is increased.[20]

While it may be rare for cyberbullying to be the sole or main cause of suicide, it should not detract from the fact that it has potential to act as 'the last straw' in causing a child or teenager to take their life. Who among us, even if psychologically sturdy, wouldn't be distressed to find messages on our phone from someone saying that they wanted you dead? That was the reality for a seventeen-year-old Balbriggan boy, whose mother linked his suicide to cyberbullying.[21]

Forms of Cyberbullying and their Ill-Effects

Evidence is emerging that the impact of cyberbullying differs depending on the forms of cyberbullying experienced by young people. Those aged eleven to sixteen reported that bullying by pictures and video clips had a greater impact on them than carried out via phone calls, texts or chat rooms.[22] In fact, the latter methods were found to have less of an effect than traditional bullying, while email and instant messaging were reported to have the same effect as traditional bullying.

The fact that cyberbullying is felt more acutely when pictures and video clips are used is perhaps to be expected in view of the potential for fast and wide distribution of the images, as in the 'Slane Girl' case. Only future research can tell whether this method is chosen knowing it will create maximum upset or hurt or whether the camera simply presents itself as a more expedient way to reach victims.

We must not lose sight of the fact that there are young people who see cyberbullying simply as divorced from reality and are not bothered by it.[23] Even our own study showed that one-third of boys (31%) and one-quarter of girls (25%) are of the opinion that cyberbullying does not cause them any upset.[24] As one fifteen-year-old reported: 'It doesn't matter. I don't mind it but some people might.' Another boy the same age had this to say: 'It doesn't bother me because these bullies are more cowardly than regular bullies.' Yet another remarked: 'In my opinion, bullying is a fact of life and cyberbullying is a safe way for it to manifest itself.' A sixteen-year-old respondent was of the opinion that 'if someone is stupid enough to bully you over the internet instead of actually saying it to you, you have nothing to worry about'. Yet it is possible that teenagers who are unaffected by cyberbullying are those who are not subjected to other stressful life events, and have effective coping strategies and good social support in place.

Victims of Both Cyber and Traditional Bullying

As discussed, cyberbullying very often occurs in the context of traditional bullying. There is growing evidence that children subjected to both forms of bullying – referred to in the literature as 'poly-victims' or 'global victims' – have been found to have significantly poorer self-esteem and higher loneliness scores and are at an increased risk of depression and loneliness.[25] They are also at a greater risk of suicide. An international retrospective analysis of forty-one young people aged thirteen to eighteen who took their own lives has shown that 78% of teens who committed suicide were bullied both at school and online, while 17% were subjected to online bullying only. A mood disorder was also reported in 32% of the teens, and symptoms of depression in an additional 15%. From these results John LeBlanc concluded that 'cyberbullying is a factor in some suicides but almost always there are other factors such as mental illness or face-to-face bullying'.[26] As one of the teenagers in our own study remarked, 'Cyberbullying made me upset because I also had depression which makes it worse'.[27]

Consequences of Cyberbullying Others

Children and adolescents who cyberbully only, like their traditional counterparts, experience many difficulties compared with uninvolved peers. They have been found to feel unsafe at school and uncared for by their teachers, and to have a high level of headaches. In addition, they have been found to have a high level of conduct problems, hyperactivity, frequent smoking, drunkenness and low pro-social behaviour.[28]

Consequences of Being a Cyberbully-Victim

Young people who both cyberbully and are bullied (cyberbully-victims) have consistently been found, along with their traditional counterparts, to be most at risk of psychiatric and psychosomatic

61

problems.[29] Compared with pure victims and pure bullies, they have the highest rates of anxiety, depression and school absences.[30] For example, bully-victims aged ten to seventeen were found to be six times as likely to report emotional distress as a result of being targeted than pure victims.[31]

Cause and Effect of Emotional and Behavioural Difficulties Related to Cyberbullying

As most of the research referred to in this chapter is based on cross-sectional studies, causality cannot be taken as given in respect of relationships between cyberbullying and psychosomatic symptoms and depression. It has been argued, for example, that the loneliness and depressive mood found in many cyber-victims may have led them to seek anonymous relationships on the internet, triggering their vulnerability to victimisation.[32] Longitudinal studies are needed to track the direction of the psychosocial problems over time in order to infer causality with greater confidence.

One longitudinal study, although not yet replicated in relation to cyberbullying, has shown the destructive powers of bullying.[33] For example, when young people presented with depression, suicide ideation and bullying (as bullies, victims or both), they were found to be suffering from more psychiatric problems four years later than those who had reported only depression or suicidality or bullying behaviour in the absence of depression or suicide ideation. The results of the above study finds strong support in the case of Conor Cusack, a former Cork hurler who, talking to Brendan O'Connor on RTÉ's *Saturday Night Show* about his experiences of school bullying, left little doubt that it has the potential to drive victims to suicide.[34]

In view of recent research indicating that cyberbullying places children, especially those who experience other stressful life events, at serious risk of psychosocial problems, loneliness, low self-esteem, depressive moods, lower educational achievements, anger, aggression, rule-breaking behaviours, self-harming, suicide ideation and suicide, every effort must be made at a national level to provide the members of school communities with the ability to prevent, identify and deal with cyberbullying. How this can be done will be addressed in the next two parts of the book.

Chapter 5: Key Facts

- Cyberbullying and its impact on children and teens shares many of the health problems, psychosocial and emotional difficulties with traditional bullying, the most common being anxiety, fear, loneliness, erosion of self-esteem, poor concentration and reduced grades, distrust of friends, depression, self-harming, thoughts of suicide and even suicide.
- The method of cyberbullying has been shown to determine its impact, with offensive and embarrassing pictures and video clips having the greatest negative effect.
- A combination of cyber and traditional bullying increases the risk of loneliness, depression and suicide.
- Poor social skills and social problems, such as withdrawing from friends and erosion of self-esteem, can lead to greater internet usage in order to meet needs for social interaction. This can place the victim at risk of further bullying.
- Cyberbullies risk conduct and behavioural problems and substance abuse.
- Cyberbully-victims are the most troubled of all the bully status groups, with both emotional and behavioural problems. They are most at risk of depression and suicide.
- While there are some issues around cause and effect, longitudinal studies suggest that cyberbullying can have short- and long-term consequences.

Notes

1. G. Gini and T. Pozzoli, 'Association Between Bullying and Psychosomatic Problems: A Meta-Analysis', *Pediatrics* 123 (2009): pp. 1059–66; C. Mills, S. Guerin, F. Lynch, I. Daly and C. Fitzpatrick, 'The Relationship Between Bullying, Depression and Suicidal Thoughts/Behaviour in Irish Adolescents', *Irish Journal of Psychological Medicine* 21 (2004): pp. 131–3.
2. R. S. Tokunga, 'Following You Home From School: A Critical Review and Synthesis of Research on Cyberbullying Victimisation', *Computers in Human Behaviour* 26 (2010): pp. 227–87.
3. R. M. Kowalski, S. P. Limber and P. W. Agatston, *Cyberbullying: Bullying in the Digital Age* (London: Wiley-Blackwell, 2012).
4. M. L. Ybarra, J. K. Mitchell, J. Wolak and D. Finkelhor, 'Examining Characteristics and Associated Distress Related to Internet Harassment: Findings from the Second Youth Internet Safety Survey', *Pediatrics* 118.4 (2006): pp. 1169–1177.

5. K. J. Mitchell, M. Ybarra and D. Finkelhor, 'The Relative Importance of Online Victimisation in Understanding Depression, Delinquency and Substance Use', *Child Maltreatment* 12 (2007): pp. 314–24.

6. Ken Foy, 'Gardaí to Investigate Slane "Sex" Pictures', *The Herald* (20 August 2013).

7. Ibid.

8. B. K. Fredstrom, R. E. Adams and R. Gilman, 'Victimisation Difficulties During Adolescence', *Journal of Youth and Adolescence* 40 (2011): pp. 405–15.

9. M. O'Moore, 'No Safe Haven From Bullying Epidemic', *The Sunday Business Post* (25 August 2013).

10. T. Beran and Q. Li, 'The Relationship Between Cyberbullying and School Bullying', *Journal of Student Wellbeing* 1 (2007): pp. 15–33; D. L. Hoff and S. N. Mitchell, 'Cyberbullying: Causes, Effects, and Remedies', *Journal of Educational Administration* 47.5 (2008): pp. 652–65; V. Sleglova and A. Cerna, 'Cyberbullying in Adolescent Victims: Perception and Coping', *Cyberpsychology: Journal of Psychosocial Research on Cyberspace* 5.2 (2011): art. 4; M. O'Moore, 'Cyberbullying: The Situation in Ireland', *Pastoral Care in Education* 30 (2012): pp. 209–23.

11. L. Corcoran, *Traditional Bullying and Cyberbullying at Post-Primary School Level in Ireland: Countering the Aggression and Buffering its Negative Psychological Effects*, unpublished PhD (Trinity College, University of Dublin, 2013).

12. B. Holfeld and M. Grabe, 'An Examination of the History, Prevalence, Characteristics and Reporting of Cyberbullying in the United States', *Cyberbullying in the Global Playground: Research from International Perspectives*, Li, Cross and Smith, eds (London: Wiley-Blackwell, 2012).

13. Beran and Li (2007), op. cit.

14. J. W. Patchin and S. Hinduja, 'Bullies Move Beyond the Schoolyard: Preliminary Look at Cyberbullying', *Youth Violence and Juvenile Justice* 4 (2006): pp. 148–69.

15. M. L. Ybarra, M. Diener-West and P. J. Leaf, 'Examining the Overlap in Internet Harassment and School Bullying: Implications for School Intervention', *Journal of Adolescent Health* 41 (2007): 542–50.

16. Corcoran (2013), op. cit.

17. A. Sourander, A. B. Klomek, M. Ikonen, J. Lindroos, T. Luntamo, M. Kosklainen, T. Ristkari and H. Helenius, 'Psychosocial Risk Factors Associated With Cyberbullying Among Adolescents', *Arch Gen Psychiatry* 67 (2010): pp. 720–8.

18. O. Erdur-Baker and I. Tannkula, 'Psychological Consequences of Cyberbullying Experiences Among Turkish Secondary School Children', *Procedia-Social and Behavioural Sciences* 2 (2010): pp. 2771–6; C. Fong-Cing, L. Ching-Mei, C. Chiung-Hui, H. Wen-Yun, F. Tzu and P. Yun-Chieh, 'Relationships Among Cyberbullying, School Bullying, and Mental Health in Taiwanese Adolescents', *Journal of School Health* 83 (2013): pp. 454–62.

19. June Shannon, *Irish Clinical News* (22 July 2013), p. 32

20. J. C. LeBlanc, 'Cyberbullying Only Rarely the Sole Factor Identified in Teen Suicides', paper presented at the American Academy of Paediatrics, National Conference and Exhibition, New Orleans (20 October 2012).

21. G. Naughton, 'Mother Links Son's Suicide to Cyberbullying', *The Irish Times* (4 April 2014).

22. P. K. Smith, J. Mahdavi, M. Carvalho, S. Fisher, S. Russell and N. Tippett, 'Cyberbullying: Its Nature and Impact in Secondary School Pupils', *The Journal of Child Psychology and Psychiatry* 49 (2008): pp. 376–85.

23. R. Ortega, P. Elipe, J. A. Mora-Merchan, J. Calmaestra and E. Vega, 'The Emotional Impact on Victims of Traditional Bullying and Cyberbullying: A Study of Spanish Adolescents', *Journal of Psychology* 217 (2009): pp. 197–204.

24. O'Moore (2012), op. cit.

25. A. Brighi, G. Melotti, A. Guarini, M. L. Genta, R. Ortega, J. A. Mora-Merchan et al., 'Self-Esteem and Loneliness in Relation to Cyberbullying in Three European Countries', *Cyberbullying in the Global Playground: Research From International Perspectives*, Q. Li, D. Cross and P. K. Smith, eds (London: Wiley-Blackwell, 2012): pp. 32–56; P. Gradinger, D. Strohmeier and C. Spiel, 'Motives for Bullying Others in Cyberspace: Austria', Li, Cross and Smith, eds, pp. 263–84.

26. LeBlanc (2012), op. cit.

27. Corcoran (2013), op. cit.

28. Sourander, Klomek, Ikonen, Lindroos, Luntamo, Kosklainen, Ristkari and Helenius (2010), op. cit.

29. Ibid.

30. R. M. Kowalski, S. P. Limber and P. W. Agatston, *Cyberbullying: Bullying in the Digital Age* (London: Wiley-Blackwell, 2012).

31. Ybarra and Mitchell (2007), op. cit.

32. D. Olenik-Shemesh, T. Heiman and S. Eden, 'Cyberbullying Victimisation in Adolescence: Relationships with Loneliness and Depressive Mood', *Emotional and Behavioural Difficulties* 17 (2012): pp. 361–74.

33. A. B. Klomek, M. Kleinman, E. Altschuler, F. Marrocco, L. Amakawa and M. S. Gould, 'High School Bullying as a Risk for Later Depression and Suicidality', *Suicide and Life-Threatening Behaviour* 41 (2011): pp. 501–16.

34. *Saturday Night Show*, RTÉ (15 February 2014).

6

COPING WITH CYBERBULLYING

In view of the substantial negative impact of cyberbullying on the mental and physical health of children and adolescents, finding effective coping strategies to reduce the emotional distress and stop the bullying is of paramount importance.

All cyberbullied children and adolescents will try to somehow buffer the impact of the bullying and, if at all possible, to respond in a way that will put an end to it. However, some will be more successful than others. Their responses will vary from doing nothing, telling a friend or a parent, reporting the abuse to the service provider or getting really angry.

The actions of bystanders can also make a difference to the impact and outcome of a cyberbullying incident. For example, 'I told the person to stop or they would get a piece of me' and 'I make sure the person goes to a guidance counsellor'.[1]

Unfortunately, research into coping strategies for cyberbullying is still in its infancy. Of the studies conducted so far, most have investigated only the use but not the success of the various coping strategies. Thus the insights regarding the effectiveness of different strategies are still limited, although there is some evidence to indicate that the impact of cyberbullying can be lessened by the application of beneficial coping strategies.[2]

The main types of coping strategies identified to date in relation to cyber-victimisation are:

- Supportive strategies: seeking help from friends, peers, family, carers and teachers
- Aggressive coping: retaliation, confrontation, physical attacks, verbal threats
- Avoidant and emotion-focused strategies: avoidance, escape, anger, helplessness, self-blame, hopelessness, accepting cyberbullying as part of one's life
- Cognitive coping: responding assertively, solution focused, using reason, analysing the bullying incident

- Technical coping: applying technical skills to give protection from further attacks, e.g. changing settings, passwords or mobile phone numbers, blocking the sender, reporting abuse to service providers, and saving the evidence of the abusive messages or images.

Gender Differences

Boys have been found to use more active and physical retaliatory behaviour, whereas girls tend to use more passive and verbal retaliatory behaviour. For example, boys have reported, 'I watched the person and when I got him alone, I ended it' and 'I physically assaulted the bully'. Girls, on the other hand, more typically changed their own behaviour or retaliated with words. For example, 'I changed my email and screen name', 'I decided not to go online, which wasn't fair to me' and 'I sent mean messages back'.[3]

While the girls' approach may have more to recommend it than physical retaliation, Hoff and Mitchell point out that the strategies put victims in a position of changing their behaviour. This may temporarily deter the bully but it is unlikely that it will discourage them from acting again. Also, verbal retaliation may perpetuate the cyberbullying with retaliatory messages that are likely to prolong the bullying.

Social Coping

The emerging research indicates that seeking 'close support' is a highly adaptive coping strategy in relation to cyber-victimisation. Telling a friend, for example, has been reported to be the most helpful strategy, buffering the negative impact of being cyberbullied.[4] However, the support or advice from friends is not always the best and can be counter-productive, especially when it is aggressive, causing the bullying to escalate.

The alternative to confiding in friends is to turn to parents and teachers. Unfortunately, this option is rarely chosen. The reason cyber-victims do not confide as readily in their parents as in their friends is that they fear their parents will overreact, perhaps denying access to the internet or by having the relevant social networking account closed down.[5] One teenage had this to say: 'I wanted to tell my parents but I was afraid that they would never let me chat again and I know that's how a lot of other kids feel.'[6]

Victims often feel there is too much of a digital divide between their parents and themselves to allow them to understand. For example, one female victim remarked, 'They do not understand the internet and I have no desire to explain it to them time and time again …'[7]

A reason put forward for not reporting cyberbullying to teachers or school principals is the belief that they won't act on it. For example, in one study 17% of students reported a cyberbullying incident to a teacher, yet in 70% of these cases the school did not react to it.[8] One Irish pupil said, 'I went to the principal but they did nothing about it. They didn't believe me even though I took screencaps and showed it to them. They just sent me to counselling.'[9]

Victims' personal characteristics and their educational and family circumstances will also influence how and from whom the victim might seek help. Children who feel uncared for by their teachers, who feel disillusioned and distrustful of their peers, or who are from families made up of other than two biological parents, have been found to find it more difficult to share their problems. It is also to be expected that introverted children will find it more difficult to unburden themselves and share their emotions with others.[10]

Not seeking support is also undoubtedly due to a victim's feelings of guilt. As many as one in eight children have been found to feel guilty about being cyberbullied. This is perhaps not surprising in view of the risky behaviour that young people often engage in online. For example, it has been found that:

- 40% looked for new friends on the internet
- 34% added people to their friends list or address book that they have never met face to face
- 16% pretended to be a different kind of person on the internet from who they really are
- 15% sent personal information to someone that they had never met face to face
- 14% sent a photo or video of themselves to someone that they had never met face to face.[11]

It has been argued that victims give false information about themselves – such as age and sex – as a ploy to protect themselves from further victimisation.[12] However, parents and school staff can be reassured by the finding that while children and teenagers may not readily confide in adults, they are more inclined to do so when the problem has escalated to such a level that they feel they can no longer cope.[13]

Technical Coping

Technical coping is considered an active attempt at problem solving and has been found to be a very popular strategy with children and adolescents throughout Europe. The most common action is to block the aggressor, or to delete the nasty or hurtful messages. One in five have been found to stop using the internet for a while, and almost as many changed their filter or contact settings. Less than one in ten made use of the 'report abuse' button or reported the problem to someone who provides an online support (such as their internet service provider).

While blocking has been found to be the most effective of the various technical coping actions,[14] there are studies that show technical coping to be insufficient and ineffective in the long term. For example, where server administrators have been contacted they have often failed to react, allowing accounts that have slanderous and negative information to remain active. Indeed, Sleglova and Cerna report on cases where technical coping turned into disadvantages. In one case the victim ended up being expelled from a chat room by an administrator after using foul language as a result of his frustration at the failure of the administrator to deal adequately with his complaint of victimisation.[15]

A further limitation of technical coping is that the cyberbully can simply keep creating new accounts as their false accounts get blocked or deleted by the victim.

Avoidant and Emotion-Focused Coping

Online avoidance can take the form of not replying, not answering, ending a call, closing the account that is the source of the cyberbullying and creating a new one (or a new account with a new server, e.g. closing Facebook and signing up to Twitter). Instead of trying to fix the problem of cyberbullying, a sizeable proportion (24%) of victims have been found to take this approach, hoping that the problem will go away by itself. However, as researchers point out, this may not be such a bad response considering how easy it is to aggravate bullying by one's actions.[16]

When considering avoidance as a coping strategy, it is necessary 'to distinguish between consciously choosing to avoid the cyberbullying once consideration has been given to the other possible options versus "closing one's eyes" with an accompanying intense feeling of helplessness'.[17]

Those who chose online avoidance can, of course, reinforce it further by avoiding or ignoring the cyberbully in real life and pretending not to be upset or dwell on the problem. However, whereas ignoring may be an effective strategy following a single incident, other more active strategies are needed should the incidents increase in frequency and severity.[18]

It is of note that it is not uncommon for individuals to utilise problem-solving coping strategies first and foremost, and to switch to emotion-focused coping when the situation is perceived as unchangeable. Thus, the longer one experiences cyberbullying, the more likely it is that emotion-focused strategies will be used.[19]

It should also be borne in mind that the feelings of helplessness, which so often characterise victims, may have as much to do with their own failed efforts at intervening (or indeed those of their parents, friends or teachers) as they have to do with their fatalistic attitude at the outset.

Coping Skills of Irish Children

It is encouraging that nearly two-thirds of Irish victims shared their victimisation with their friends, family or a staff member, thus using social coping as a strategy.[20] However, boys were much less inclined to use this form of coping. Like their European counterparts,[21] few Irish victims chose to talk to their teachers about their cyber-victimisation.

Worrying was the significant proportion of children and adolescents (almost one in ten) who had told no one. With no form of close social support, these children would be at particular risk of the negative impacts of cyber-victimisation. The reluctance to seek support may explain why so many pupils in our study called for 'schools to make it easier for victims to report and gain support'. Here are some of their comments:

71

'There is not much schools can do, except make sure there is always a counsellor for students to talk to.'
'Schools can set up class meetings to talk about bullying and allow students to share their feelings once a week.'
'Encourage students to speak up if they are being cyberbullied so they know it is not embarrassing.'

The fact that almost one-third of pupils sent back an angry message reflects the poor awareness of best practice for coping with cyber-attacks. Qualitative responses also reflected the frequency with which victims used physical aggression to avenge themselves.

In a more recent study of 2,474 Irish pupils aged between twelve and nineteen, half of those who admitted to having been cyberbullied reported that they were effective in stopping it.[22] Many of them reported using a combination of coping strategies in order to avoid further incidents of bullying. The more popular strategies were close support, active ignoring and assertiveness, as compared with distal advice (advice centres), helplessness and retaliation. However, consistent with international findings, boys were inclined to use retaliation, whereas girls chose close support as their preferred coping strategy.

In examining which coping strategies were most successful in reducing the negative emotions of cyber-victimisation, we found that the victims who had attempted problem-focused coping had fewer health complaints than those who tried to retaliate or avoid the problem. Close support and assertive coping were related to increased psychological well-being. Helpless (passive) coping, on the other hand, was related to negative mental health. Retaliation was associated with increased depressive symptoms.

Whereas aggressive coping has been found to be ineffective in dealing with cyberbullying, there is evidence to show that adolescents who employed this form of coping were less likely to be cyber-groomed. Cyber-groomers were found to use chat rooms, social-networking sites, instant messenger and websites and blogs, and girls were at particular risk of being cyber-groomed.[23]

Cyberbullying and Bystanders

There is a growing recognition of the significant role played by bystanders in bullying situations, whether traditional or cyber. Their behaviour has been shown to be critical in cushioning the impact of victimisation for the victim,[24] so much so that their role has been referred to as 'the invisible engine in the cycle of bullying'.[25]

It is undisputed that most young children and adolescents, irrespective of age, are witness to bullying and contribute in different ways to support it. Research has shown that 20–30% of preadolescents and adolescents encourage the bully, acting as assistants or reinforcers. Actively intervening to stop bullying and helping the victim was found to characterise no more than 20%, whereas another 20–30% were silent witnesses to bullying incidents.[26]

Nancy Willard makes the distinction between harmful bystanders – those who encourage, cheer on and support the bully or watch the bullying from the sidelines, but do nothing to intervene or help the victim – and helpful bystanders – those who try to stop the bullying, protest against it, provide support to the target, or tell an adult.[27]

In a study of cyberbullying among adolescent bystanders (aged eleven to eighteen), it was found that negative bystander behaviour occurs more often in cyberspace than in real life.[28]

Critically, the study also showed that heightened empathy (both cognitive and emotional) is associated not only with active but also passive bystanding behaviours. This finding demonstrates that empathic responsiveness, while important for active defending behaviour among adolescents, is not enough to prompt intervention in a bullying situation. Active defending, therefore, requires not only high levels of empathic responsiveness but also high levels of perceived social self-efficacy. Thus, as the researchers point out, other personal abilities (such as communication skills, social problem-solving abilities and coping skills) distinguish active and passive defenders. Several reasons have already been put forward as to why passive observers fail to take supportive actions in real life, the main ones being:

- They do not know how to intervene
- They are fearful of becoming the next victim

- Their lack of skills and competence in defending may cause even more problems
- Conflicting attitudes, social norms or moral ideas (loyalty to individual group).[29]

These reasons have found strong support in Irish pupils. A recent doctoral study showed that lack of confidence, fear of making things worse, the need to be accepted by their group, the risk of losing friends and the fear of being bullied oneself were the most common motives preventing bystanders from intervening in a bullying situation. However, pupils found it easier to intervene when they were considerably older than the perpetrator(s).[30]

As physical size and strength or social prowess is not required for cyberbullying, it has been hypothesised that bystanders are more likely to take part in cyberbullying than are bystanders of traditional bullying.[31] However, others are of the view that the beliefs children and adolescents hold about the online world is the most fundamental factor contributing to their actions when they witness cyberbullying.[32] The more negative a belief the young person holds (i.e. a disregard for 'netiquette', with the online world being one where everyone can say whatever they wish, which amounts to a moral disengagement), the more likely it is that they will participate in cyberbullying by cheering on the cyberbully. On the other hand, a positive belief (i.e. acceptance of the moral standards of cyberspace) prompts the young person to leave the online environment, or to solve the problem by helping or befriending the victim or reporting the incident to someone in authority.

A finding of great consequence for parents and teachers is that direct requests for help from victims trigger supportive bystander behaviour.[33] This means that as the online environment denies bystanders the opportunities to witness victims' emotional responses, a direct request for help might overcome the tendency for bystanders to remain passive.

When our Irish study asked 'What did you do when you saw someone getting cyberbullied?' we found that only a minority (1%) of pupils who admitted to witnessing cyberbullying alerted a teacher or a parent. Typical answers were 'I did nothing at all' or 'I stayed out of it'. However, one in twenty pupils (6% girls and 4% boys) said they tried to stop the bullying. Boys tended to use some form of verbal or physical aggression. One pupil remarked, 'I told the bully to "f" off'. Another said, 'I beat them up'. Yet another stated, 'I knocked him out'.[34] Such responses demonstrate how cyberbullying can escalate and how a cyberbully can quickly become a cyber-victim.

In addition to the bystanders who intervened directly there was another 7% (9% girls and 5% boys) who were willing to support the victim, stating, for example, 'I helped the person who was getting bullied and taught him how to respond'. One in twenty reported that they were upset at what they witnessed but did nothing to stop it. A minority of pupils (1%) said they joined in the cyberbullying, and sadly another 3% (2% girls and 5% boys) admitted to having fun watching it.

These findings on the coping strategies of children and adolescents when subjected to and witness to cyberbullying point to a strong need to educate our young people about the effectiveness and ineffectiveness of the various coping strategies, so that they can better alleviate the emotional impact and put a stop to bullying behaviour. How this can best be done by teachers and parents will be addressed in the next two sections of the book.

Chapter 6: Key Messages

- Social, technical and cognitive coping are regarded as effective strategies, whereas aggressive coping serves to escalate the bullying.
- When cyberbullied, boys are less inclined to seek social support by talking to friends, parents or teachers.
- Technical coping, while effective, can backfire.
- Passive coping is associated with the most mental health problems.
- Bystanders are critical in buffering the impact of cyberbullying.
- Empathy alone does not explain active/helpful bystander behaviour.
- Direct requests for help from victims have been found to be effective, especially in relation to cyberbullying, as bystanders are not able to judge the emotional response of those targeted.

Notes

1. M. O'Moore, *Understanding School Bullying: A Guide for Parents and Teachers* (Dublin: Veritas, 2010).
2. K. Machmutow, S. Perren, F. Sticca and F. D. Alsaker, 'Peer Victimisation and Depressive Symptoms: Can Specific Coping Strategies Buffer the Negative Impact of Cybervictimisation?', *Emotional and Behavioural Difficulties* 17 (2012): pp. 403–20; S. Perren, L. Corcoran, H. Cowie, F. Dehue, D'J. Garcia, C. McGuckin, A. Sevcikova, P. Tsatsou and T. Vollink, 'Tackling Cyberbullying: Review of Empirical Evidence Regarding Successful Responses by Students, Parents, and Schools', *International Journal of Conflict and Violence* 6.2 (2012): pp. 283–93.
3. D. L. Hoff and S. N. Mitchell, 'Cyberbullying: Causes, Effects, and Remedies', *Journal of Educational Administration* 47 (2009): pp. 652–65.
4. Machmutow, Perren, Sticca and Alsaker (2012), op. cit.
5. Ibid.
6. J. W. Patchin, 'Overview, Significance and Impact of Cyberbullying in the United States and Beyond', Presentation at the First International Cyberbullying Congress, Berlin (11 September 2013).
7. V. Sleglova and A. Cerna, 'Cyberbullying in Adolescent Victims: Perception and Coping', *Cyberpsychology: Journal of Psychosocial Research on Cyberspace* 5.2 (2011): art. 4.
8. Hoff and Mitchell (2009), op. cit.
9. L. Corcoran, *Traditional Bullying and Cyberbullying at Post-Primary School Level in Ireland: Countering the Aggression and Buffering its Negative Psychological Effects*, unpublished PhD (Trinity College, University of Dublin, 2013).
10. A. Sourander, A. B. Klomek, M. Ikonen, J. Lindroos, T. Luntamo, M. Kosklainen, T. Ristkari and H. Helenius, 'Psychosocial Risk Factors Associated With Cyberbullying Among Adolescents', *Arch Gen Psychiatry* 67 (2010): pp. 720–8; F. Dehue, C. Boman and T. Vollink, 'Cyberbullying: Youngsters' Experience and Parental Perception', *Cyberpsychology and Behaviour* 11 (2008): pp. 217–332.
11. S. Livingstone, L. Haddon, A. Görzig and K. Ólafson, *Risks and Safety on the Internet: The Perspective of European Children* (London: LSE, 2011).
12. C. Katzer, D. Fetchenhauer and F. Belschak, 'Cyberbullying: Who Are the Victims?: A Comparison of Victimisation in Internet Chat Rooms and Victimisation in School', *Journal of Media Psychology* 21 (2009): pp. 25–36.
13. Hoff and Mitchell (2009), op. cit.
14. Livingstone, Haddon, Görzig and Ólafson (2011), op. cit.
15. Sleglova and Cerna (2011), op. cit.
16. Livingstone, Haddon, Görzig and Ólafson (2011), op. cit.
17. Sleglova and Cerna (2011), op. cit.
18. R. S. Tokunga, 'Following You Home From School: A Critical Review and Synthesis of Research on Cyberbullying Victimisation', *Computers in Human Behaviour* 26 (2010): pp. 277–87.
19. T. Vollink, C. A. W. Bolman, F. Dehue and N. C. L. Jacobs, 'Coping with Cyberbullying: Differences Between Bully-Victims and Children Not Involved in Bullying', *Journal of Community and Applied Social Psychology* 23 (2013): pp. 7–24.
20. M. O'Moore, 'Cyberbullying: The Situation in Ireland', *Pastoral Care in Education* 30 (2012): pp. 209–23.

21. Livingstone, Haddon, Görzig and Ólafson (2011), op. cit.
22. L. Corcoran (2013), op. cit.
23. S. Wachs, K. D. Wolf and C. C. Pan, 'Cybergrooming: Risk Factors, Coping Strategies and Associations with Cyberbullying', *Psicothema* 24.4 (2012): pp. 628–33.
24. G. Huitsing, R. Veenstra, M. Sainio and C. Salmivalli, '"It Must Be Me" or "It Could Be Them?": The Impact of the Social Network of Bullies and Victims on Victims' Adjustment', *Social Networks* 34 (2012): pp. 379–86.
25. S. W. Twendlow, P. Fonagy, F. C. Sacco, M. L. Giesm and D. Hess (2001), cited in J. Barlińska, A. Szuster and M. Winiewski, 'Cyberbullying Among Adolescent Bystanders: Role of the Communication Medium, Form of Violence, and Empathy', *Journal of Community and Applied Social Psychology* 23 (2013): pp. 37–51.
26. C. Salmivalli, K. Lagerspetz, K. Bjorkqvist, K. Osterman and A. Kaukiainen, 'Bullying as a Group Process: Participant Roles and Their Relations to Social Status Within the Group', *Aggressive Behaviour* 22 (1996): pp. 1–15.
27. N. Williard, 'An Educator's Guide to Cyberbullying', Centre for Safe and Responsible Internet Use (2007), www.cyberbullying.org/docs/cpct.educators.pdf (accessed 1 September 2014).
28. J. Barlińska, A. Szuster and M. Winiewski, 'Cyberbullying Among Adolescent Bystanders: Role of the Communication Medium, Form of Violence, and Empathy', *Journal of Community and Applied Social Psychology* 23 (2013): pp. 37–51.
29. R. Thornberg, 'A Classmate in Distress: Schoolchildren as Bystanders and Their Reasons for How They Act', *Social Psychology of Education* 10 (2007): pp. 5–28.
30. K. L. H. Finnegan, *Bullying in School: Listening to the Bystander*, unpublished PhD (Trinity College, University of Dublin, 2012).
31. R. M. Kowalski, S. P. Limber and P. W. Agatston, *Cyberbullying: Bullying in the Digital Age* (London: Wiley-Blackwell, 2012).
32. Q. Li and T. Fung, 'Predicting Student Behaviours in Cyberbullying', *Cyberbullying in the Global Playground: Research from International Perspectives*, Q. Li, D. Cross and P. K. Smith, eds (London: Wiley-Blackwell, 2012).
33. H. Machackova, L. Dedkova, A. Sevcikova and A. Cerna, 'Bystanders' Support of Cyberbullied Schoolmates', *Journal of Community and Applied Social Psychology* 23 (2013): pp. 25–36.
34. M. O'Moore (2012), op. cit.

PART TWO

Cyberbullying and School

CYBERBULLYING: WHAT SCHOOLS CAN DO

The ill-effects that can arise from cyber-victimisation, as shown in Chapter 5, requires that every effort is made on a national scale to prevent and counter cyberbullying. As cyberbullying behaviour, whether activated inside or outside of school, tends to have its roots in social relationships formed at school, schools are well placed in helping with prevention.

Due to the significant overlap between cyber and traditional bullying (see Chapter 2) it is imperative that we apply the same measures to tackling cyberbullying as have been developed to prevent and counter 'real-life' bullying.[1] Essentially, both forms of bullying rely on the same principles: intention to hurt, repetition, imbalance of power and helplessness. If young people learn to refrain from traditional bullying, the chances are high that they will also refrain from online bullying. Schools will, of course, have to introduce specific modules so that children are better able to engage in safe and healthy cyber-behaviour.

I have argued for some time now, on the basis of my own and international research, that the whole school community approach is the most effective in preventing and managing traditional bullying. There is now evidence that such an approach substantially reduces the levels of cyberbullying, in parallel with reductions in traditional bullying.[2]

It is therefore encouraging that the whole school community approach has been endorsed by the Department of Education and Skills in their *Plan of Action on Bullying* and that it has been validated further by their new *Anti-Bullying Procedures*, published in September 2013.[3] While the new *Anti-Bullying Procedures* uses the term 'a school wide approach', rather than a 'whole school community approach' the programmes are essentially the same in that they reach out to all the members of the school community – the staff, pupils, families and those members of the wider community – who come into daily direct contact with school pupils:

School bus drivers, school traffic wardens and local shopkeepers are to be encouraged to play a positive role in assisting schools to counter bullying behaviour by reporting such behaviour to parents and/or to the school as appropriate. Through such approaches, a network is formed.[4]

Thus, to prevent and counter cyberbullying the whole school community approach needs to be the method of choice for schools, with an additional emphasis on modules that specifically address cyberbullying. Support for embedding cyberbullying in this approach is also found in the recent *Guidelines on Preventing Cyberbullying in the School Environment.*[5]

The guidelines found that in tackling cyberbullying, the elements central to a whole school community approach were made up of four main pillars of action:

1. Building and reviewing annually the school policy and practice so that bullying in all its forms is consistently and effectively addressed
2. Building an understanding of and skills for dealing with bullying
3. Building a positive and supportive school culture
4. Building collaborative partnerships between staff (teaching and non-teaching), students, families, the wider community and external agencies and professional bodies.

Developing, Revising and Reviewing the Anti-Bullying Policy and Practices

Key to an effective whole school community approach is a school policy and practices that send out a strong message that the school finds all forms of bullying unacceptable and that it is committed to taking action whenever it is witness to or receives a report of bullying. A policy that discourages all forms of bullying and encourages positive social skills and the reporting of bullying behaviour facilitates staff to take consistent and effective action, and will help to build the necessary confidence that is needed for schools to follow through on its reports of bullying.

Too often, parents and the wider community are not aware of their school's anti-bullying policy. It cannot be stressed often enough that building awareness and consistent implementation of the school policy can only be achieved if all parents, students and staff are clear on the procedures for preventing, detecting, reporting and responding to incidents of bullying.

However, to enhance understanding of and commitment to the school policy and practices, they need to be developed in collaboration with all members of the school community. It is very important that young people especially, as stressed in the Ombudsman for Children's Report,[6] are consulted because this will give them a greater sense of ownership of their school's anti-bullying policy. To promote the policy, all available forms of communications, both offline and online, should be used – a view that is supported in the new *Anti-Bullying Procedures*.

In Ireland, in accordance with the Education (Welfare) Act 2000, all schools are required to have an anti-bullying policy within the framework of their overall code of behaviour. However, the degree to which schools have so far developed and implemented a comprehensive anti-bullying policy and further followed this up by regularly revising or renewing the policy has varied considerably.[7] Recently, Jacky Jones reported that only three out of ten schools that she contacted had a bullying policy on their website. Two of these were based on the 1993 guidelines and she was unable to download the third.[8]

It is clear then that school boards of management and education centres need to endeavour to have their anti-bullying policies updated in order to meet with the recommendations of the new *Anti-Bullying Procedures*. It is recommended that policies make specific reference to cyberbullying as well as relational bullying, sexual bullying and identity-based bullying, including in particular homophobic and transphobic bullying. In addition, they need to include all grounds of harassment under the Equal Status Acts. This means taking account of all 'one-off' negative acts, which should have the effect of preventing an escalation of negative behaviours.

Integrating Cyberbullying into Anti-Bullying Policy
The first step in developing a policy that relates specifically to cyberbullying is to have students complete an anonymous questionnaire about bullying behaviour. Questions specific to

cyberbullying will provide useful information about the forms and methods most frequently used to bully peers or indeed staff. It will also provide important information about the level of cyberbullying in the different year groups and whether there are any differences between the boys and girls. In addition, it will determine the extent to which cyberbullying occurs during or out of school hours.[9]

Setting the Rules for Cyber-Behaviour

The school's rules for cyber-behaviour should be written into the policy so that all members of the school community are clear about expectations and consequences. In setting the rules that are to apply to children and adolescents, pupils' views need to be sought in keeping with best practice of class control and management.[10] Agreement then needs to be sought on the sanctions that are to be applied in the case of a breach.

An example of possible rules for cyber-behaviour might be:

Our school will not tolerate:
1. Sending or displaying offensive messages or pictures
2. Using obscene language
3. Harassing, insulting or attacking others
4. Damaging computers, computer systems or computer networks
5. Violating copyright laws
6. Using others' passwords or accounts
7. 'Hacking' into others' folders, work or files for any reason
8. Intentionally wasting limited resources, including printer ink and paper.[11]

Recording Cyberbullying Incidents

As has been recommended in the new *Anti-Bullying Procedures*, it is vital that schools keep a record of all bullying incidents, inclusive of cyberbullying. While it may be seen as an inconvenience, it will help staff to see whether there is a pattern of behaviour emerging with individual students. It would also benefit staff in talking to parents about their child's bullying behaviours. Parents can so easily become defensive, not believing that their child would commit the alleged offence. To be able to show parents that the alleged offence may not

84

be the first one will help to gain their co-operation when introducing a programme of intervention.

Most importantly, keeping records of anti-bullying incidents will provide staff with valuable information when reviewing the effectiveness of the school's interventions, and the role that age and gender play in the outcomes. In addition, keeping a good record of incidents will help schools answer any queries that may arise as a result of potential legal action due to parental dissatisfaction with the school's intervention strategies for their child or teen.

The new *Anti-Bullying Procedures* include a template for staff to record bullying behaviour. However, a student assessment form[12] would also help in gaining a greater understanding of the motives for the cyberbullying behaviour and in finding the most appropriate intervention. For example, was the child or teen aware that they were bullying? Did they cyberbully alone or in a group? Such a form would also shed light on the motivation for the cyberbullying. For example, was it to right a wrong, or was it due to anger, revenge, boredom, entertainment, to impress, to be admired, to create fear, embarrassment, intimidate and/or hurt others?

Investigation of Incidents

The new *Anti-Bullying Procedures* endorse the need for schools to investigate reports of bullying, recognising that the primary aim of an investigation is 'to resolve any issues and restore, as far as is practicable, the relationships of the parties involved rather than to apportion blame'. Importantly, the procedures, similar to the Massachusetts anti-bullying law,[13] accept that even if the reports are anonymous they should be investigated.

I have heard staff say that they do not entertain anonymous reports and I believe this is short-sighted, as every opportunity should be taken to prevent and correct any bullying that may be causing a hostile environment for their pupils. Swedish research has shown that consistent recording of reported bullying reduces bullying by 30%.[14] Of course, no disciplinary action should be taken against a student solely on the basis of an anonymous report.[15]

Should the result of an investigation not satisfy the concerns of individual parents it is important that, as recommended in the *New*

Procedures, schools advise parents of their right to make a complaint to the Ombudsman for Children. Making this recommendation reflects the school's commitment to resolving bullying. It will also help to avoid unnecessary adversarial and costly litigations.

Intervention

Acknowledging that international and national research continues to evolve as to the effectiveness of intervention strategies, the new *Anti-Bullying Procedures* state that each school must decide on the intervention method(s) best suited to their circumstances. In view of the limitations of punitive approaches to address bullying,[16] it is advisable that schools consider taking a restorative rather than a punitive approach, which would involve direct sanctions, commonly ranging from verbal reprimands, meeting with parents and removal from class to suspension and expulsion.

Essentially, disciplinary approaches have three main purposes:

1. To impress on the perpetrator(s) that what they have done is unacceptable
2. To deter the perpetrator(s) from repeating that behaviour
3. To signal to other pupils that the behaviour is unacceptable and to deter them from doing it.[17]

While holding pupils to account for their behaviour, restorative approaches also help them to develop empathy and to take responsibility for their actions, as they are asked to put right the harm that they have caused. Harsh consequences, on the other hand, can create an authoritarian environment in which students will feel less motivated and connected. Restorative approaches, with an emphasis on recognition of hurt and application of constructive and rehabilitative measures, are increasingly being used in schools and are showing great promise.[18]

There will, however, be occasions when direct sanctions need to be applied and thus it is important that those sanctions be included in the policy. As it is not unusual for serious incidents of cyberbullying to involve the Gardaí, it is advisable that this is mentioned as part of the direct sanctions.

Examples of direct sanctions include:

- Violations of the rules for internet use will result in a temporary or permanent ban on internet/computer use
- Parents/carers will be informed
- Additional disciplinary action may be added in line with existing practice on inappropriate language or behaviour
- When applicable, police or local authorities may be involved
- If necessary, external agencies such as social networking or email member sites may be contacted and informed.[19]

It is to be noted that restorative approaches may not be appropriate for schools where there is an intake of students with moderate to severe learning difficulties. A case study has shown that empathy-creating strategies were seen as unworkable in such environments, whereas direct sanctions providing a 'black and white' set of consequences were more effective.[20]

Supporting Those Involved in Cyberbullying

How a school supports those involved in cyberbullying incidents speaks volumes about their attitude towards bullying, such as how seriously they take bullying as a whole and cyberbullying in particular. Chapter 5 showed that the impact of cyberbullying can be as great, if not greater, than traditional bullying and that if combined with traditional bullying the hurt may be even greater still. In Chapter 3, the risk factors for those who bullied were discussed. For schools to reduce the impact on victims, bullies and bully-victims, they must have strategies in place for their aftercare.

Sensitivity should be given to the social and emotional needs of victims, for example whether or not they feel able to meet with the bullies and share their playtime or learning with them. Peer mediation is no longer recommended for victims due to the power imbalance between the perpetrator and the victim. If there is more than one perpetrator the power imbalance increases. There is also the added risk that the bully can blame the victim for the bullying.[21] Victims should have the option of counselling and should be made aware of the action that has been taken to discipline the bully.

87

Provision for interventions for children who have bullied or who have been bully-victims should also be made in order to reduce their tendency towards bullying. Possible interventions are discussed in my book, *Understanding School Bullying: A Guide for Parents and Teachers*.

Bullying Outside of School

A source of increasing concern is cyberbullying that takes place outside of school grounds. A fourteen-year-old boy summed up a common attitude when he said, 'It's none of their business what goes on outside of school, they are paid to teach, not to interfere in our personal lives. So long as bullying is happening outside of school it is none of their business.'[22]

While schools may feel it is not their responsibility,[23] I believe any behaviour that causes a hostile environment for a pupil should be addressed by the school. The Massachusetts anti-bullying law, for example, states that bullying is prohibited

> at a location, activity function or programme that is not school-related, or through the use of technology or an electronic device that is not owned, leased or used by a school district or school, if the bullying creates a hostile environment at school for the victim, infringes on the rights of the victim at school or materially and substantially disrupts the education process or the orderly operation of a school.[24]

Criminalising Cyberbullying

It has been argued that introducing specific laws to regulate cyberbullying will create unnecessary criminal records for young people. This need not be the case if the same procedures are adopted as those pertaining to juvenile offences, namely that young people guilty of a serious offence would have an interview with a juvenile liaison officer and be given a warning and, if regarded as beneficial to them, they would be referred for appropriate psychological support to deal with their inappropriate behaviour. This would be the best way to facilitate early intervention, especially as children who engage in bullying are at risk of long-term substance abuse and anti-social behaviour into adulthood, leading to criminal convictions.[25] To allow the offending behaviour to go unchallenged without some remedial attention would be irresponsible.

The Oireachtas Joint Committee of Transport and Communications' *Report Addressing the Growth of Social Media and Tackling Cyberbullying* was satisfied with existing legislation for dealing with cyberbullying.[26] However, should it come to pass that a specific law is necessary to curb cyberbullying, then it would be necessary for schools to place considerable emphasis on children's legal literacy, as currently they tend not to appreciate their potential for attracting criminal liability.[27]

For example, young people tend to think that instant messages are private and transitory. They also tend not to fear punishment, as they believe adults do not supervise their cyberspace. Even where there are laws in place, as in Ireland (see 'Some Law on Cyberbullying', page 165), it has been found that young people do not know which laws apply to their behaviour when they cyberbully.

In addition to the steps outlined, an excellent checklist for schools, determined to significantly reduce bullying and avoid the possibility of legal challenges, are the recommendations made by Murray Smith to the working group of the Action Plan on Bullying.[28] They are as follows:

1. Make the policy freely and easily available to the school's students, parents and guardians, and staff.
2. Examine the anti-bullying policy and, if found necessary, update at least once every two years. The new *Anti-Bullying Procedures* give recommendations every year.
3. The creation of the policy, its examination and, if necessary, updating, should be as a result of consultation between the school's students, parents and guardians, and staff.
4. The policy should contain a definition of bullying, with a non-exhaustive list of examples.
5. The policy should clearly state that such behaviour is unacceptable, and will be dealt with by the school in relation to particular times, places, and the use of particular equipment, i.e. computers.

6. The policy should outline the procedure to be followed when a student, or a person on the student's behalf, makes a complaint of bullying.

7. The policy should outline the sanctions that may follow, up to and including suspension or expulsion, if an investigation of a complaint of bullying finds in favour, completely or partly, of the student alleged to have been bullied.

8. The policy should make it clear that all allegations made in writing will be responded to in writing within fourteen days, in which details will be given of the investigation and sanction-imposing procedures, including when the relevant person or body will meet the complainant or those acting on the complainant's behalf. Such meetings should take place within a reasonable time frame. If this is not possible, sufficient and complete reasons for this should also be given in writing.

9. The policy should make it clear that the student accused of bullying is entitled to be informed of the details of the allegations made against him or her, and given the right to respond to the allegations. It should be also made clear that any attempt to intimidate or influence the student alleged to have been bullied, or any witnesses, may also lead to the imposing of sanctions.

10. The policy should make it clear that while an allegation of bullying is being investigated, all the relevant parties observe confidentiality.

11. The policy should make it clear that there should be an absence of bias and partiality in the person or persons investigating allegations of bullying, and, if there is a complete or partial finding in favour of the allegations, in the person or body imposing sanctions. In order to ensure this, any investigation should be separated from the sanction-imposing process. If any sanction to be imposed is of a serious nature, the person found to have bullied is entitled to address the sanction-imposing person or body.

12. The policy should make it clear that the student, or the person complaining on the student's behalf, has the right to be informed – within a reasonable time frame and in writing – of

the result of the investigation, the reasons for the result and, if the investigation upholds some or all of the complaint, what sanctions were imposed and the reasons for their imposition.

13. The policy should make it clear that if any person or body imposing sanctions departs from those listed in the policy, that person or body gives sufficient and complete reasons in writing for doing so.

Building Key Understandings, Skills and Competences

All members of the school community need awareness-raising programmes to help them understand how to prevent, identify and deal effectively with cyberbullying. Inspired by the National Strategy for Violence Prevention in the Austrian public school system,[29] this means that schools need to arrange for all its members to acquire:

- A commonly shared definition of cyberbullying
- Commonly shared principles on how to cope with cyberbullying
- Commonly agreed measures to substantially reduce cyberbullying.

The pupils

To deepen the understanding of cyberbullying and the significant role pupils can play in preventing it, the topics that need to be embedded into the curriculum are:

- Cyberbullying and the different forms it can take
- The methods that are used to cyberbully
- The school's policy and rules in respect of cyberbullying
- Participant roles in cyberbullying and associated risk factors
- The damaging effects of cyberbullying for the victims and bully-victims
- The damaging effects of cyberbullying inclusive of their reputation, e.g. friendships, future employment prospects
- Internet safety
- The myths of anonymity
- The principles of netiquette (digital citizenship)
- Coping strategies
- The legal consequences and risks of prosecution.

Also, in view of the relationship found between bullying and the lack of social skills, assertiveness, self-esteem, empathy and moral perceptions of bullying, there need to be curricular activities to provide pupils with opportunities to develop these skills and behaviours central to forming healthy friendships and relationships. In Austria, for example, as part of their National Strategy for Violence Prevention, class time is taken up with training students to feel responsible when something negative is going on, and to react in a way that is likely to improve the situation. Also, all students are trained to recognise their own emotions and the emotions of others and to cope with these in a positive, non-aggressive way. In recognising that there are children who are victimised easily because of their non-assertive behaviour, all students are trained how best to react when others are picking on those children.

Both the Social Personal Health Education (SPHE) and the Relationships and Sexuality Programme (RSE) have the scope to provide much of the critical understanding, skills and competences referred to above, but only if the programmes are given the attention they deserve. However, a module specific to cyberbullying that is appropriate for the different school-going age groups is still lacking. Until such time as it is developed, hopefully by the National Council for Curriculum and Assessment (NCCA), there are useful learning resources that can be used in class time. See page 183 in this book for useful resources.

In addition to curricular activities, there will be children and teenagers who need help to overcome the causative factors in cyberbullying that implicate inadequate patterns of parenting and adult role modelling, and it is here that schools should seek assistance from outside professional agencies, rather than trying to contain problems with deep roots outside the school environment.

Enhancing children's technical and safety skills needs to be, in particular, an ongoing process in view of the fast-moving electronic communication technology. A meta-analysis of interventions to prevent cyber abuse has shown the effectiveness of educating pupils about technical and safety strategies in preventing, responding to and reporting incidents of cyberbullying.[30] Understandably, the emphasis that needs to be placed on internet safety will depend on the skill level of staff. Should it be lacking, assistance needs to be sought from an external agency, although very good programmes have been developed for different age groups by the Irish Internet Safety Awareness Centre.

Staff

The delivery of the curricular topics necessary to enhance the understanding of cyberbullying among students and the implementation of effective strategies requires schools to assess the capacity of their staff. While the contribution of school guidance counsellors can make up for the lack of pre-service training for teachers, professional development opportunities must be provided for staff to help them grow in confidence and to be better able to prevent, identify and deal with the many and new forms of bullying that will arise. It has been shown, for example, that only 40% of staff in second-level schools have had training on cyber safety, and less than one-third (28.9%) on cyberbullying.[31]

To deal with cyberbullying incidents more effectively, analysis of the European guidelines for preventing cyberbullying in the school environment found that teachers would benefit from a deeper understanding of group dynamics and conflict management skills.[32] In particular, it is vital that they learn to distinguish between bullies who bully others in order to attain a particular goal (such as dominance), bully-victims who have vented their anger as a result of difficulties they have in managing their emotional response or hostile attributional biases, and victims who cannot easily defend themselves. In addition, and in keeping with other international prevention programmes, they need to be able to:

- Support and empower victims
- Stop negative and reinforce positive behaviours in bullies
- Foster competence in emotional regulation among bully-victims
- Stimulate parents to co-operate with the school in reducing aggression and bullying.

Parents

Providing information for families has been shown to be very effective in reducing the level of traditional bullying among children.[33] So there

93

is no reason to believe it should be any different for cyberbullying. Given that cyberbullying occurs more often outside of school or youth centres, developing parents' understanding is vital in order to give them the necessary confidence to talk to their children about it. All too often one hears parents refer to their children as 'digital natives' and to themselves as 'digital immigrants' and it is this divide that prevents many parents from discussing matters relating to internet safety and cyber behaviour with their children.

Many parents misguidedly believe that by supervising and monitoring their children's internet use they are preventing their child from being bullied or from bullying others. It has been shown, however, that 64% of nine- to sixteen-year-olds access the internet in their friends' houses and have social-networking accounts unknown to their parents.[34] Parents need to strike a balance between supervising and monitoring their child's internet use and promoting trust, self-discipline and open communication. This will be made easier when parents are made aware, through educational programmes, of the different modes of communication and how each of these can be used by children to cyberbully others. Parents must also be made aware of how they can contact mobile and internet service providers and help their children in reporting problems, securing their privacy settings or indeed blocking senders of abusive messages or images.

Parents often do not realise that even though their children are technically skilled they may not know how to use the technology in safe ways. This is especially true of younger children. Parents need to be made aware, therefore, of the signs of cyberbullying, and to look out for their children becoming withdrawn, moody, depressed, visibly upset or angry. They need to support their children during this time and also to report the situation to the school for their attention.

If schools do not have their own staff to create the awareness raising campaigns, they should invite professionals to the school to talk to the parents. The school website can also be used to good effect. For example, links can be provided to:

- Useful resources, such as the Family e-Safety Kit (saferinternet. org) and the *Get With It!* series (internetsafety.ie), which provide

information for parents on new media technologies, social-networking sites and filtering technologies
- Online courses (e.g. cybertraining4parents.org/ebook/)
- External agencies, such as Childline (childline.ie), Parentline (parentline.ie) and ABC's Teen Forum (tacklebullying.ie), where parents and children can seek information and advice
- Counselling services, if affected by cyberbullying.

Sending out letters or newsletters with information on cyberbullying, both off- and online, is also an excellent way to reach parents. It is strongly recommended that such information includes:

- Definition of cyberbullying
- Examples of cyberbullying and how to report it at school
- Appropriate online netiquette and the importance of treating others well online
- Guidelines for protecting one's privacy online, as well as the privacy of others
- Tips on responding to cyberbullying (e.g. ignoring, blocking or warning)
- Safe use of social-networking sites, as well as other social media and how to report abusive behaviour
- When to notify the Gardaí
- Possible parental liability for their children's online behaviour
- Who to contact for more information or assistance.

Building Collaborative School–Family Relations

Tempting as it may be for schools to refer cyberbullying issues back to parents, it should be recognised that cyberbullying is often rooted in school even though the incidents may happen outside it. Schools must, therefore, take leadership and encourage all members of their community to tackle cyberbullying. Analysis of European guidelines for cyberbullying showed that parents are often overlooked when such problems arise in schools. It is recommended that teachers develop closer links with parents and contact them when concerned. Similarly, parents need to be encouraged to report any concerns they may have about cyberbullying to the school.

Pupils also need to be empowered to report to staff and parents when they are subjected to bullying. Our Irish study showed that only 8% of girls and 5% of boys told an adult at school about being cyberbullied. While 50% of girls shared the problem with friends, only 20% of boys did so.[35] That boys crave support was strongly reflected in their qualitative statements. They called especially for schools to do more to encourage them to report cyberbullying. One thirteen-year-old boy, for example, said: 'I think teachers should get close to the students so that they will be more open to tell their problems. Every teacher should have a letter box so if any student wants to tell them about a bully they can.' A fourteen-year-old boy said: 'Make sure there is someone at the school that the students can talk to and trust.'

Schools need to work harder for their school community to recognise that there is no shame in reporting, that the problem lies with the aggressor and that the sooner the cyberbullying is addressed the sooner it will stop. To achieve this, teachers, parents and students must work together to make cyberbullying prevention a shared responsibility. Thus, the school must be open about bullying in all its forms and regularly invite views from its members, especially when reviews of the school's policy and practices are conducted. The days when schools denied that bullying was a problem in their community should be long gone.

To make reporting as easy as possible, different reporting routes should be made available. For pupils, one or more of the following systems should be available:

- Bully boxes
- Confidential web-based reporting systems
- 'Befrienders' or 'buddies', who are stationed at a known locality every day
- Think books (stories and pictures which stimulate children's thinking skills and which can be used to discuss peer relationships and peer support)
- Peer mentors
- Text or email systems
- Confidential phone numbers
- School counsellors or drop-in facilities to talk with home–school workers/mentors.[36]

However, such systems are only of value if pupils have confidence that their concerns will be met with prompt and sensitive action, and that their situation will not be made any worse. That schools are unresponsive to requests for help is sadly evident by the recent account of a sixteen-year-old who reported that 'one of her classmates came out as a lesbian in school and is still being bullied. Teachers know, but feel powerless to intervene. The girl's friends became the targets of bullies. The girl informed the principal but he did not act on it.'[37]

To empower parents to report incidents of cyberbullying it would be helpful for schools to have their reception staff trained in their procedures, so they are clear about the steps that need to be taken when parents contact the school regarding bullying incidents. In addition, schools need to ensure that their staff:

- Are sensitive to the emotional needs of the parents when they make contact
- Act promptly and take action that does not make the situation worse for the child
- Take actions to agreed time frames and report progress to parents
- Make parents aware of what further action can be taken should they feel their concerns have not been properly addressed. A model letter informing them of their complaints procedures would meet this need.[38]

Building a Positive and Supportive Environment

A positive and supportive environment that promotes diversity and respect for individual differences and supports restorative discipline models will provide a feeling of safety. As a result, it will encourage open communication and positive relationships among pupils, staff and parents. Crucially, it promotes a feeling of connectedness to the school, which helps to reduce the risk of bullying.

Evidence shows that when students feel like they belong and are cared for by their schools they are also more likely to achieve academically and hold positive attitudes towards themselves and others. They are also less likely to drop out of school and to engage in health-risking behaviours.[39] On the other hand, not feeling safe at school and cared for by their teachers has been shown to be a significant risk factor for bullying and/or cyberbullying others.[40]

A caring and supportive school culture will also contribute to students becoming more willing to report and intervene when they witness bullying incidents. Seeing staff respond consistently and effectively to bullying will provide students with greater confidence and skills to do likewise.

To build school connectedness requires enhancing positive interactions among pupils, as well as engaging pupils in school life through positive school and extracurricular activities. Practical tips for building a positive school culture and climate is to be found on page 43 of the new *Anti-Bullying Procedures*. It requires that all members of the school community model and display respectful behaviour at all times. This means acknowledging desired behaviour and consistently challenging discriminatory and derogatory language and behaviour.

An understanding of restorative approaches also needs to be provided, especially for parents. All too often when restorative approaches, such as the no blame approach, are applied in response to bullying incidents, a critical stance is taken by parents and indeed sometimes staff and students. For example, a fourteen-year-old pupil remarked: 'Schools should be allowed to cane students who they find participating in any kind of bullying. A yard of stick is better than a mile of talk.'[41] Schools would be well advised, therefore, to provide information evenings and/or newsletters to explain the value of restorative approaches. Confirmation of its effectiveness is to be found in an evaluation of the use and effectiveness of anti-bullying strategies in schools commissioned by the UK Department of Education.[42] However, while highly effective, the report cautioned that staff training was an important consideration.

Schools should not be afraid, however, to suspend or expel students when the bullying is persistent and after restorative measures have been tried. Indeed, in not doing so it may contradict their own procedures.

Chapter 7: Key Messages

- To prevent and counter cyberbullying, attention also needs to be given to traditional bullying, because the majority of children are involved in both forms.
- Schools can affect change by implementing the whole school community approach.
- The whole school community approach involves four pillars of action: building an anti-bullying policy; strengthening understanding, skills and competences for all members of the school community; encouraging school and family collaboration; and developing a supportive social environment.
- The views of staff, pupils and parents need to be sought when developing, revising and renewing their anti-bullying policies and practices.
- To encourage disclosure of cyberbullying, schools must act on all requests for help in a manner that does not make the situation worse for victims.
- In dealing with the perpetrators, restorative approaches should be used in preference to the more punitive direct sanctions.
- Schools need to make their members, in particular pupils and parents, aware of external agencies and professionals who can provide additional advice, guidance and support.

Notes

1. J. Riebel, R. S. Jaeger and U. C. Fischer, 'Cyberbullying in Germany: An Exploration of Prevalence, Overlapping with Real Life Bullying and Coping Strategies', *Psychology Science Quarterly* 51 (2009): pp. 298–314.
2. D. Olweus, 'Cyberbullying: An Overrated Phenomenon?' *European Journal of Developmental Psychology* 9 (2012): pp. 520–38.
3. Department of Education and Skills, *Action Plan on Bullying* (2013), http://www.education.ie/en/Publications/Education-Reports/Action-Plan-On-Bullying-2013.pdf; Department of Education and Skills, *Anti-Bullying Procedures for Primary and Post-Primary Schools* (2013), http://www.education.ie/en/Publications/Policy-Reports/Anti-Bullying-Procedures-for-Primary-and-Post-Primary-Schools.pdf.
4. *Anti-Bullying Procedures for Primary and Post-Primary Schools.*
5. M. Välimäki, A. Almeida, D. Cross, M. O'Moore, S. Berne, G. Deboutte, T. Heiman, D. Olenik-Shemesh, M. Fulop, H. Fandrem, G. Stald, M. Kurki and E. Sygkollitou, *Guidelines for Preventing Cyberbullying in the School Environment: A Review and Recommendations*, http://sites.google.com/site/costiso801/ (2012). The guidelines resulted from a COST (European Co-operation in Science and

Technology) action on cyberbullying and had ten researchers, of which I was one, to examine already nationally published guidelines in twenty-eight European countries plus Australia.

6. Ombudsman for Children's Office, *Dealing with Bullying in Schools: A Consultation with Children and Young People* (Ireland, 2012).

7. M. O'Moore and P. Stevens, eds, *Bullying in Irish Education: Perspectives in Research and Practice* (Cork: Cork University Press, 2013).

8. J. Jones, 'Anti-bullying policy is clear, so schools should act on it', *The Irish Times*, Health and Family, 20 May 2014.

9. Examples of such questionnaires can be found in B. Holfeld and M. Grabe, 'An Examination of the History, Prevalence, Characteristics and Reporting of Cyberbullying in the United States', *Cyberbullying in the Global Playground*, Li, Cross and Smith, eds (London: Wiley-Blackwell, 2012) and A. Katz, *Cyberbullying and E-Safety: What Educators and Other Professionals Need to Know* (London: Jessica Kingsley, 2012).

10. D. Fontana, *Psychology for Teachers*, in association with British Psychological Society (London: Palgrave, 1995).

11. Department for Children, Schools and Families, *Safe to Learn: Embedding Anti-Bullying Work in Schools* (Nottingham: DCSF Publications, 2007).

12. Such as that of B. C. Trolley and C. H. Hanel in *Cyber Kids, Cyberbullying, Cyber Balance* (Thousand Oaks, CA: Corwin, 2010).

13. Massachusetts Anti-Bullying Law, http://www.malegislature.gov/Laws/SessionLaws/Acts/2010/Chapter 92.

14. E. Flygare, G. M. Frånberg, P. Gill, B. Johansson, O. Lindberg, C. Osbeck et al., *Evaluation of Anti-Bullying Methods* (Stockholm: Swedish National Agency for Education, 2011).

15. Massachusetts Anti-Bullying Law, op. cit.

16. K. Rigby and S. Bauman, 'How School Personnel Tackle Cases of Bullying: A Critical Examination', *The Handbook of Bullying in Schools: An International Perspective*, S. Jimerson, S. Swearer and D. Espelage, eds (New York: Routledge, 2009), pp. 455–68.

17. Department for Children, Schools and Families, *Safe to Learn: Embedding Anti-Bullying Work in Schools* (2007), www.teachernet.gov.uk/publications.

18. M. Kent and S. Fallon, 'Bullying: Tools for Teachers', *Bullying in Irish Education: Perspectives in Research and Practice*, M. O'Moore and P. Stevens, eds (Cork: Cork University Press, 2013).

19. *Safe to Learn*, op. cit.

20. F. Thompson and P. K. Smith, *The Use and Effectiveness of Anti-Bullying Strategies in Schools*, Research Brief DFE-RB098 (2011), http://www.education.gov.uk/publications/.

21. E. Roland, 'Mobbingens psykologi: Hva kan skolen gjøre?' (Oslo Universitetsforlaget, 2014).

22. M. O'Moore, 'Cyberbullying: The Situation in Ireland', *Pastoral Care in Education* 30 (2012): pp. 209–23.

23. L. Corcoran, *Traditional Bullying and Cyberbullying at Post-Primary School Level in Ireland: Countering the Aggression and Buffering its Negative Psychological Effects*, unpublished PhD (Trinity College, University of Dublin, 2013).

24. Massachusetts Anti-Bullying Law, op. cit.
25. A. Sourander, A. B. Klomek, M. Ikonen, J. Lindroos, T. Luntamo, M. Kosklainen, T. Ristkari and H. Helenius, 'Psychosocial Risk Factors Associated With Cyberbullying Among Adolescents', *Arch Gen Psychiatry* 67 (2010): pp. 720–8.
26. Houses of Oireachtas Joint Committee on Transport and Communications, *Report Addressing the Growth of Social Media and Tackling Cyberbullying* (2013), www.oireachtas.ie/parliament/media/Report-on-Social-Media-July-2013-Website.pdf.
27. M. Campbell and A. Zavrsnik, 'Should Bullying be Criminalised?' *Cyberbullying Through the New Media*, P. K. Smith and G. Steffgen, eds (London: Psychology Press, 2013).
28. *Action Plan on Bullying* (2013), op. cit.
29. C. Spiel and D. Strohmeier, 'National Strategy for Violence Prevention in the Austrian Public School System: Development and Implementation', *International Journal of Behavioural Development* 35 (2011): pp. 412–18.
30. F. Mishna, C. Cook, M. Saini, M. J. Wu and R. MacFadden, 'Interventions to Prevent and Reduce Cyber Abuse of Youth: A Systematic Review', *Research on Social Work Practice* 21 (2011): pp. 5–14.
31. Corcoran (2013), op. cit.
32. M. O'Moore, D. Cross, M. Valimaki, A. Almeida, S. Berne et al. 'Guidelines for Preventing Cyberbullying: A Cross-National Review', *Cyberbullying Through the New Media*, Smith and Steffgen, eds (London: Psychology Press, 2013).
33. D. P. Farrington and M. M. Ttofi, *School-Based Programmes to Reduce Bullying and Victimisation*, Campbell Systematic Reviews (Oslo: The Campbell Collaboration, 2009).
34. B. O'Neill, S. Grehan and K. Ólafson, *Risks and Safety for Children on the Internet: The Ireland Report*, EU Kids Online (London: LSE, 2011).
35. O'Moore, 'Cyberbullying: The Situation in Ireland' (2012), op. cit.
36. *Safe to Learn: Embedding Anti-Bullying Work in Schools* (2007), op. cit.
37. P. McGuire, 'What Are Your Children Learning About Being Gay?', *The Irish Times* (11 March 2014).
38. *Safe to Learn: Embedding Anti-Bullying Work in Schools* (2007), op. cit.
39. C. A. McNeely, J. M. Nonnemaker and W. R. Blum, 'Promoting School Connectedness: Evidence from the National Longitudinal Study of Adolescent Health', *Journal of School Health* 72 (2002): pp. 138–46.
40. Sourander, Klomek, Ikonen, Lindroos, Luntamo, Kosklainen, Ristkari and Helenius, 'Psychosocial Risk Factors Associated With Cyberbullying Among Adolescents' (2010), op. cit.
41. O'Moore, 'Cyberbullying: The Situation in Ireland' (2012), op. cit.
42. Thompson and Smith (2011), op. cit.

WHAT TEACHERS CAN DO

In the same way as teachers are key to preventing and countering traditional bullying, so they are central to tackling cyberbullying. They are in an excellent position to be both proactive (picking up on any tell-tale signs and giving class time to strengthening the pupils' understanding, skills and competences) and reactive (acting decisively and consistently on requests for help from victims, bystanders, parents or anonymous reports of cyberbullying, even if the cyberbullying behaviour has occurred outside of school). It is to be expected that when cyberbullying behaviours, like traditional bullying behaviours, are not acknowledged or effectively dealt with by staff, they will persist and even increase over time. Reflecting this view, one of our Irish pupils commented: 'The school should have a better vice-principal than we do because we get into trouble for stopping a fight, and then the real bully gets away.'[1]

The level to which children and adolescents are bothered by their online experiences and the degree to which they use social-networking sites means that they need to become more astute at preventing and coping with behaviours that place them at risk of being cyberbullied, of cyberbullying others or both.

While it has been argued that the school curriculum is already stretched, the DES has pointed out in their new *Anti-Bullying Procedures* that there is space within the teaching of all subjects to:

- Foster an attitude of respect for all
- Promote value for diversity
- Address prejudice and stereotyping
- Highlight that bullying behaviour is unacceptable.

Specific to cyberbullying, the new *Anti-Bullying Procedures* add that 'the curriculum provides opportunities for students to consider their attitudes and their safety when online and make informed decisions about their health, personal lives and social development in this context'.[2] There is evidence that where countries have fully embedded internet safety in the curriculum, young people have become more digitally aware and proficient.[3]

Teachers need to challenge normative opinion that there is little schools can do to combat cyberbullying. It is not uncommon, for example, to hear pupils state that 'There is nothing schools can realistically do, because they do not have control over what kids do in their own time, or on the internet.'[4] However, if children are introduced at a young age to regular class discussions on cyberbullying, they will be in a stronger position to recognise the signs, cope with the negative behaviours in an effective manner and seek help if necessary.

Children's narratives have shown that many children do not even know that cyberbullying is a form of bullying, and this clearly makes it difficult for them to seek help.[5] While parents have a responsibility to educate their children about safe internet use, there is greater certainty that a minimum standard will be reached if teachers provide the required understanding and competence to tackle cyberbullying in class time.

To compensate for there being no specific module on cyberbullying, there are good learning resources that have been designed to be delivered as part of the CSPE and SPHE curriculum (such as ThinkB4Uclick, //:Be SAFE_Be WEBWISE:// for Primary and Post-Primary Schools, Watch Your Space and most recently the #Up2Us Anti-Bullying Kit). The Anti-Bullying Campaign website also has a variety of anti-bullying exercises for use with children at both primary and post-primary level. The Garda Secondary Schools Programme, *Connect with Respect*, is another good resource and is excellent for introducing pupils to criminal liability in respect of accessing or posting offensive material on the internet.

In addition to Ireland's Office for Internet Safety, the UK Safer Internet Centre also have a wealth of resources that can be used to deliver lessons on internet safety and digital citizenship for children and teenagers (three to nineteen years of age). The adventures of Smartie the penguin, for example, helps to educate younger children (three to seven) about clicking and seeking adult advice and supervision while navigating the internet; while the adventures of Kara, Winston and the Smart Crew are designed for eight- to eleven-year-olds. There are companion lesson plans that work in association with the story. A complete set of resources are available from kidsmart.org.uk. The site also provides excellent resources for the older age groups (for example, 'sexting', 'so you got caught naked?', 'ask.fm online safety guidance' and 'video chat and webcams').

Classroom Management

Important as curriculum activities are for the prevention of cyberbullying, the quality of classroom management is also vital. A study conducted in Ireland has shown that almost one-third of Irish pupils have been bullied by teachers and over a quarter of students have admitted to bullying their teachers.[6] There is strong evidence to indicate that the level of bullying is significantly lower in classrooms where:

- Every pupil feels cared for by their teachers
- Individual favouritism is avoided
- Teachers teach to a high standard
- Teachers monitor their pupils' work and behaviour closely in class and during break times
- Teachers consistently intervene when there is inappropriate behaviour.[7]

Essentially, every class needs authoritative leadership to improve social cohesion and limit relational tension between pupils, and also pupils and teachers. It is important that the principles of authoritative adult leadership extend outside of the classroom to all areas of the school, such as the corridors and play areas. It is also essential that pupils see their teachers engage in positive social behaviour at all times. To expect pupils to exercise empathic responses, be respectful and tolerant, requires that school staff, teaching and non-teaching, model these behaviours. There should be no room for double standards as this diminishes credibility in dealing with bullying.

Teacher Intervention
Responding to children's concerns
In spite of good internet safety education and policy, occasions will arise when children have concerns related to their experiences of

cyberbullying that need to be addressed by teachers. Younger children especially may have concerns relating to sexual images or websites that they may have come across on the internet. Five per cent of nine- to ten-year-olds and 25% of fifteen- to sixteen-year-olds have seen sexual images on websites, 34% of which were bothered or upset by it.[8] Concerns may also relate to hurtful and sexual messages that they have received. Whereas 81% of children report feeling upset by such experiences, of those only 9% clicked a 'report abuse' button. If children raise concerns it is because they are looking for help. Research shows that the more positive and supportive the school climate is, and the more pupils feel cared for by their teachers, the greater is the likelihood that they will seek help from staff.[9]

In a school that is supportive there should be no shame for teachers in not having the necessary IT skills to advise their students of better safety measures. If a teacher feels, for example, that they do not have the necessary skills, they should express their approval to the student for bringing the concerns to their attention, as this will encourage and reinforce them in seeking support, and then refer them to a colleague who can help them at a technical level. In certain instances it may be necessary to help pupils report illegal or offensive material to the relevant internet provider or social-networking site. Helping pupils to address their concerns is of critical importance in cases where, through gentle probing, it may come to light that a pupil does not feel they can approach their parents for fear of punishment (e.g. being denied internet access) or as a result of their parents' lack of digital literacy skills.

Similarly, if a teacher lacks the confidence to deal with reports of cyberbullying, they should ensure that the pupils get the necessary help from someone who has the training and the skills to both intervene and to provide or arrange for the aftercare and support required. It is to be expected that schools with a school guidance counsellor can play a central role in supporting class teachers in the prevention and intervention of cyberbullying.[10]

Responding to Tell-Tale Signs
As highlighted in Chapter 6, teachers are, unfortunately, most often the last to learn of a pupil's victimisation, due to the reluctance of

children to disclose their problems for reasons ranging from fear of reprisal to shame that they may have bullied back or been drawn into embarrassing behaviour to appease the bully. It is vital, therefore, that teachers are proactive in responding to the tell-tale signs that are characteristic of pupils who are suffering from being cyberbullied:

- Behaviour that is out of character
- Begins to miss school
- Few or unusual friendships
- Is often alone
- Receives laughter and ridicule from classmates
- Loss of interest in school or underperforming in academic or extra-curricular activities.

If you suspect depression and you feel it is inappropriate to approach the suspected victim directly, you should approach their friends or the class representative to see if they have any information to confirm your suspicions. In a school advocating good school–family collaboration (as outlined in Chapter 7), contacting parents should also be considered an option.

If all you are left with is your own suspicions, approaching the child in question is nonetheless worthwhile. The way the pupil responds to your approach should provide confirmation of your initial concerns – perhaps that they are unfounded or indeed that they have been resolved. Such a proactive step is recommended practice in suicide prevention.[11]

Should the child admit to being cyberbullied, the teacher is then to proceed in the manner laid down in their school's anti-bullying policy, using the school's standardised recording template. It is important that teachers:

- Listen carefully to the victim, giving them plenty of time to tell their version of events
- Take notes and details of any cyber evidence (e.g. emails, voicemails, text messages, picture or video clips, screen grabs)
- Allay fears and provide reassurance
- Ensure the victim's safety, which may involve informing parents, school guidance teachers and external specialist agencies

- Negotiate confidentiality, referring to the school's policy when deciding whether or not confidentiality can be offered to the victim
- Keep in contact with the victim.

Making the Intervention

Apprehending the alleged perpetrator of a cyberbullying incident is generally no different to apprehending a traditional bully, but once again the steps taken should follow the school's anti-bullying policy. In the event of the necessary steps not being included in the policy, it is important that teachers:

- Remain calm
- Talk with the victim first and then the perpetrator(s)
- Express disapproval of the inappropriate behaviour and not the person, and state respectfully and firmly that the bullying must stop
- Do not divulge the identity of who brought the incident to your attention. It is sufficient to say that the incident has come to the school's attention. If anonymous, remind them of the school's obligation to respond to anonymous reports
- Assure the perpetrator that their side of the story will be heard before a decision is made
- Take notes using the school's standardised template as included in Appendix 3 of the new *Anti-Bullying Procedures*
- If a group of pupils have cyberbullied another pupil it will be necessary to weaken the bond between the group
- Contact the parents to reinforce the collaborative approach to tackling bullying
- If the cyberbullying or its overlap with traditional bullying has not been resolved within twenty school days, as recommended by new *Anti-Bullying Procedures*, you need to make a referral to the principal or deputy principal.

Response Options

The methods of intervention to be decided on when cyberbullying has been confirmed should again be those that are set out in the school's anti-bullying policy. Even when corrective action is eventually taken, it is to be hoped that a restorative approach has been used at least initially in preference to direct sanctions. The more commonly used restorative approaches are:

The No Blame approach: This is more recently referred to as the Support Group Approach, and sets out not to apportion blame but to have the perpetrator(s) take responsibility to stop the bullying. The approach has seven steps.

1. The teacher talks individually to the victim.
2. A group meeting is convened with up to eight pupils, including the perpetrator(s), and others suggested by the victim.
3. The teacher explains to the group that the bullied pupil has a problem but does not detail the specifics of the victimisation. The bullying pupil(s) do not need to admit to their involvement.
4. The teacher emphasises that all the participants in the group must take joint responsibility to make the bullied pupil feel happy and safe.
5. Each group member is encouraged to suggest a way in which they can help the victim feel happier.
6. The teacher ends the meeting by passing over the responsibility to the group for improving the bullied pupil's safety and well-being.
7. Individual meetings are held with the group members one week after the meeting to establish the success of their intervention. It is not critical if everyone has not kept to his/her intention, as long as the bullying has stopped.

Mediation: This is a technique that can help those in conflict to settle their disputes in a way that is mutually acceptable. It can be used successfully by both teachers and pupils (see peer mediation on page 116). Mediation involves encouraging the disputants to explain their problem. When each disputant is clear on how the other feels about the contentious issues, the facilitator helps the disputants to look for a way forward that is acceptable to both. It is about finding a win-win solution. However, mediation is not to be recommended when there is a significant power difference between victim and bully. For further details and an outline of the steps, see my earlier book *Understanding School Bullying: A Guide for Parents and Teachers*.

Circle time: Pupils sit in a circle and take part in a discussion of issues of concern such as aggressive behaviour and bullying. Pupils listen carefully, making eye-contact with one another while addressing the particular problems. Children learn to understand and tolerate better the feelings and views of others and, importantly, to take a problem-solving approach.

Restorative conferencing: This is a process that seeks to repair more serious harm caused between pupils, teachers and parents. It usually involves both victim and perpetrator and their parents, as well as key members of staff. They are invited to attend the conference by the facilitator and the procedure is very similar to mediation. For details on the steps involved and a case study, see *Understanding School Bullying: A Guide for Parents and Teachers*.

Aggression Replacement Training (ART): This is an intervention that trains adolescents to cope with their aggressive and violent behaviours. It has three components: Social Skills, Anger Control Training and Moral Reasoning. It has much to offer schools where there is persistent aggression, bullying and violence that are resistant to the usual discipline policies that schools have to offer. For further details on ART, refer to *Aggression Replacement Training: A Comprehensive Intervention for Aggressive Youth*.[12]

A comprehensive evaluation of the uses and effectiveness of anti-bullying strategies in schools showed that schools which had a consistent whole school restorative approach were significantly more effective in their response to bullying incidents than partially restorative and non-restorative schools.[13]

Most popular in both primary and post-primary schools were problem-solving circles (circle time). Restorative conferencing was applied to more difficult cases, where serious harm had been caused to victims and where the bullying involved school staff, parents and other members of the school community.

The following practices illustrate the range of approaches that can be used when dealing with bullying:

- Low-level bullying is resolved by small restorative meetings in the deputy head-teacher's office with the students involved
- When a more serious bullying incident is reported, the process starts with a confrontation of the student accused of bullying, who is asked: 'Why do we need this meeting?' If the student confesses and accepts responsibility, then they apologise to the victim and sign a contract promising to change their behaviour in future
- If there is no acknowledgement of bullying behaviour, then the student reports the incident by letter to their parent/carer
- If necessary, the parent(s)/carer(s) are brought into school for a meeting. If still unresolved, a restorative meeting is organised with all the students involved to discuss their differences. The most serious cases sometimes involve the police liaison officer. The objective of the restorative conference is for the bully to take responsibility for their behaviour.

In Ireland we have seen incidents of cyber-bullying where schools have resorted to expulsion.[14] It is in cases like these where restorative conferences may have proven to be more beneficial for the entire school community. It would have allowed, in particular, the parties concerned in the conferencing to move forward with increased understanding and with undoubtedly less resentment, air of bravado and support from the peer group, which so often follows a direct sanction. That is not to undermine the fact that expulsion is an appropriate instrument of sanction for schools to employ where the educational progress of others is compromised or where issues of health and safety are of concern.[15]

Similar to restorative conferencing are 'accountability circles'. Typically the school guidance teacher would arrange for these to take place with the parties involved.[16] For example, the guidance teacher would contact the parents of the victim as well as the perpetrator to ensure that they are willing and capable of making the meeting a constructive experience. The victim has the right to refuse to attend, or indeed ask for the meeting not to go ahead. However, should the victim not wish to be present it is possible to have the meeting with the victim's parent(s) or carer(s).

The victim and/or family will have the opportunity to explain how the incident impacted on them individually and as a family and what, if any, actions they would like to see to resolve the situation. The perpetrator's parents or carers are also asked to share how the incident impacted on them. Both the perpetrator and their parent(s) or carer(s) will have an opportunity to express remorse for the inappropriate behaviour. When both parties have shared their experiences they are summarised by the facilitator, and the steps to be taken to repair the harm are agreed. These steps are written down and signed by all parties in attendance, with targeted dates and responsibilities for monitoring identified. An 'accountability circle' script might look as follows:

Questions for the student offender:
- What happened?
- What were you thinking at the time?
- What have you thought about since the incident?
- Who do you think has been affected by your actions?
- How have they been affected?

Questions for the student who was harmed:
(These questions can also be asked of the parents of the parties involved)
- What was your reaction when you first saw the website/messages/ etc.?
- How do you feel about what happened?
- What was the hardest thing for you?
- How did your family and friends react when they heard about the incident?

Summarise and follow up with:
- What are the main issues?
- What do you want to happen as a result of this meeting?

Resolution/signed agreement to include:
- Restitution and/or counselling
- Safety issues
- Retaliation issues
- Follow-up meetings, if needed.[17]

It is advisable, before deciding on the intervention to take, to determine as much as possible the factors that may have triggered the cyberbullying. We know, for example, that there are factors, both at home and at school, that are related to bullying behaviour. Poor anger management and social skills, for example, may need corrective action beyond the resources of the school staff, in which case it is at this juncture that the guidance teacher may need to make referrals to external agencies. Similarly, it may be necessary to seek external professional help for victims, particularly if the victim appears very withdrawn and depressed.

Encouraging Active Bystanding

Chapter 6 highlighted the reluctance among pupils to help their peers who are subject to both cyber and traditional bullying. Teachers can play a significant role in empowering their pupils to feel responsible and take action when they are witness to cyberbullying by giving class time to this important topic. As one fourteen-year-old pupil remarked: 'I think that teachers should make it clear that pupils can come to them in confidence and that they won't tell others. Many pupils are scared that bullying will get worse because they told their teachers.'[18]

To prevent cyberbullying, the importance of netiquette when communicating and socialising online cannot be overemphasised. In Norway it has been reported, for example, that one in four teenagers forwarded pictures or videos of others without their permission.[19] The incidence of this behaviour had doubled in just two years and reflects a poor understanding of online ethical behaviour. In essence, young people need to observe the same standards of behaviour online that they do in real life. What gives them a licence to do otherwise should be a source of discussion for them. For example, there are blogs and websites (particularly suited to younger primary school children, and which can be private to an individual school and class) that help children develop internet safety skills and online etiquette; for example the Safe Social Networking Making Waves programme (www.makewav.es).

Children and teenagers would make a significant difference to the level of cyberbullying if they were taught:

- Not to forward cruel messages, photos or videos to friends, even if asked to do so by peers
- Not to gossip or spread rumours online or at school
- To support the victim by using positive comments, letters and instant or email messages
- If they know the victim, to invite him/her to spend time with them
- To tell an adult at home or at school
- To save and print the evidence to share with an adult
- To discourage the classmate who is cyberbullying, if it is safe to do so, and to make it clear you think their behaviour is wrong.

To arrive at the above behaviours, class time needs to be given to:

- Fostering empathy and perspective
- Enhancing responsibility
- Broadening the behavioural repertoire in critical social situations.

Delivering on these goals, the Austrian Violence National Prevention Programme was implemented over two hours of class time once a week for thirteen weeks. The lessons were divided into three phases: an impulse phase, a reflection phase and an action phase. During the impulse phase, students learn alternative ways to perceive, interpret and deal with critical situations using vignette stories, discussions and role-playing. The reflection unit gives both students and teachers the opportunity to reflect on learning experiences made during the impulse phase. During the action phase, in a manner similar to the new webwise #Up2Us Anti-Bullying Kit, teachers hand over responsibility to their students to develop a common activity.[20]

Most of us live by social norms, that is, we tend to follow established patterns of behaviour. Thus, we look to others to give us guidance on how to behave when in a group or cultural setting. This means we inhibit or disinhibit our behaviours constantly to fit the perceived social norm. When pupils are directed to develop a common activity, such as a campaign, they should be made aware of the social norm as a means of reducing and preventing cyberbullying. This approach emphasises what normal behaviour is, depicting the majority view, rather than issuing scare tactics or threats of punishment. It has been used successfully to change a variety of behaviours, from heavy drinking at universities to hotel behaviour and bicycle theft.[21] Most crucially, however, the approach has been shown to be very successful in reducing bullying among teenagers in the United States.[22]

While they regard themselves as individuals, adolescents are more bound by peer influence than any other developmental group. Thus, they often behave in ways that are not in accordance with their own or their family's personal attitudes. For example, during research I have come across teenagers who are of the opinion that 'people are too scared to stand up for people because it means they might lose face or popularity' or 'schools are not interested in resolving cyberbullying incidents that happen outside of school'. The social-norm approach would challenge these defeatist attitudes by presenting credible and accurate data. Attractive posters displayed strategically around the school could be used to convey a precise message that reflects the majority view, for example:

- Most of St Ann's students (nine out of ten) agree that students should always try to be friendly with students who are different
- 99% of St Joseph's students think cyberbullying is wrong.

Peer Tutoring

There are schools throughout Ireland that have demonstrated the power of peer tutoring, or youth leadership, in tackling bullying and cyberbullying. Drimnagh Castle, for example, achieved considerable media attention for the initiative of their student council to raise awareness about cyberbullying, with the slogan 'Drimnagh Castle – Let's Kick it Out'.[23] Warren Daniel, of their student council, reported that their campaign week provided the students with a great insight into the lack of knowledge regarding internet safety and also the desire of students to engage with their peers as opposed to attending adult-led workshops. At the end of the week, 'the whole school had a sense of achievement. Indeed, students from first year remarked … that the school felt a less intimidating place and furthermore that they could feel confident in talking to senior students on issues of bullying and indeed on other subjects as well.' This account illustrates the benefits of using pupils as experts in addressing social issues.

115

Thompson and Smith also reported that, for most schools, peer-support schemes are effective methods for dealing with bullying.[24] In the primary schools, they state that 'peer supporters can be the "eyes and ears" of the staff in the playground', while in post-primary schools, peer-support schemes are the most popular method of reporting bullying. The many types of peer-support schemes reviewed for their effectiveness were:

Peer mentoring: This supports the emotional and academic well-being of younger pupils. Mentors are trained in listening skills, empathy, body language, confidentiality and when to refer to an adult.

Peer mediation: This is a problem-solving process that encourages pupils to define the problem; identify and agree a key issue; discuss and brainstorm possible options; negotiate a plan of action and agreement; and follow up and evaluate outcomes. Mediators are trained in conflict resolution and in helping their peers resolve disputes.

Peer listening schemes: This is based on the view that pupils are more likely to tell one of their peers about problems than an adult. Listeners are older pupils and are trained in active listening skills but can also have training in counselling and restorative approaches.

Circle of friends: This is made up of volunteer pupils who are trained to befriend and support pupils who are identified as isolated or rejected by their peers, and hence vulnerable to bullying. A friendship group breaks down isolation of bullied pupils and helps them to belong.

Cyber-mentors: These are virtual peer supporters who are trained to mentor pupils online from their own or other schools using a secure website. They are available online at breaktime, after school and at weekends. Back-up and support are provided online by senior counsellors who are available at all times.

Bystander defender training: This is an intervention aimed at the group dynamics of bullying. Its aim is to turn passive bystanders into active defenders of a bullied pupil, thus providing a spontaneous peer intervention. It is, as Thompson and Smith state, the most inclusive form of peer support as all students can be trained.

Lunchtime clubs: These provide activities in a designated room for vulnerable pupils, for example, pupils with poor social skills and who are bullied. The clubs are set up by peer supporters, e.g. buddies and peer mentors who are trained to supervise activities and conduct one-to-one sessions on demand with pupils needing support.

Playleaders/sports mentors: These are older pupils who organise and support 'constructive play' for younger pupils at breaktimes in the playground. Some playleader schemes work together with other forms of peer support, e.g. buddies and befrienders.

Buddy schemes: These provide social and emotional support to vulnerable pupils and can include bullied and bullying children. Buddies can be trained in playground games, mediation skills and in a specific whole school approach (e.g. restorative practice).

Bully buster/school councillors: These are elected and are the voice of their peers in any policy development on bullying. They meet regularly with members of staff and discuss and decide on policy issues. By inviting the views of their peers on all bullying-related issues, the anti-bullying committee or school council create that all-important sense of ownership among pupils.

To get the maximum benefit from peer involvement in anti-bullying, Thompson and Smith make the following recommendations:

- In recruiting pupils, care needs to be taken to avoid drop-out. Too many can cause boredom and too few become overworked. Older age groups are preferred but sixth year students can be intimidating. Applications with a personal statement and CV are preferable to nominations to avoid a popularity contest.
- In promoting the schemes, a high profile needs to be kept through assemblies, notice boards, TV screens and the intranet. It needs also to be emphasised that peer supporters do not deal with serious bullying but will refer it on to teachers.
- In training pupils, a rolling programme will prevent gaps in provision. Opportunities for trainees to shadow experienced peer supporters should be made. Training in large groups can be counterproductive.

- Supervision requires that designated supervisors are trained with the peer supporters and that they meet regularly.
- Providing a designated space allows students to find the peer supporter and prevents them from feeling undervalued.
- Provision should be made for peer-support schemes that can work indoors and in the playground; schemes outside can refer to schemes inside if necessary.
- Senior management needs to be supportive of the peer-support schemes: this will prevent the scheme supervisors and the peer supporters from becoming demoralised.

While, as discussed, peer-mediation techniques are increasingly found to be unsuitable for tackling bullying cases due to the power imbalance between 'bully' and 'victim', it is recognised that they are effective in solving conflicts between children and teenagers of equal strength, and therefore there is a strong case for having them integrated into a whole school approach.[25]

Youth Councils in the Community

Just as student councils and peer-support schemes can be effective in tackling bullying in all its shapes and forms inside school hours, there is also evidence of the effectiveness of youth groups and youth councils outside of school. For example, County Waterford's Youth Council, the Comhairle na nÓg, developed a cyber code to combat cyberbullying. Each young person who signs up to the code receives a silicon wristband in the hope that this will strengthen the young person's commitment to the code, as well as unite the young people in Waterford in the battle against cyberbullying.

There is no doubt that anti-bullying campaigns such as this link schools and communities closer together in their campaign to tackle cyberbullying. Thus, they are deserving of much praise and support from school staff. In the same way as the Princess Diana Awards recognise anti-bullying work (e.g. this year by celebrating Student Anti-Bullying Ambassadors in the UK and Ireland), teachers can inspire and give confidence to their pupils to become agents for change outside of school and in their communities. For example, they could draw their pupils' attention to the social-norm approach so that their future campaigns, whether in or out of school, will convey messages that are positive and accurate for their target audience.

Key Messages: Chapter 8

- Teachers are key to providing, during class time, the depth of understanding that is required for pupils to prevent and counter cyberbullying.
- Teachers need to develop an authoritative classroom environment that is positive, co-operative and rewarding.
- Teachers must be quick to respond to pupils' concerns about cyberbullying and upsetting messages and images that they may come across online.
- It is vital that teachers respond and follow up on the tell-tale signs of bullying, both cyber and traditional.
- Restorative approaches are preferable to direct sanctions in addressing bullying incidents, both cyber and traditional.
- Teachers are key to encouraging active bystanding as a means to counter cyberbullying.
- Teachers should, with the help of their pupils, introduce social-norm campaigns to tackle cyberbullying.
- Teachers should encourage peer tutoring and peer-support schemes to tackle cyberbullying.
- Teachers should inspire and encourage their pupils to engage in anti-bullying work outside of school to reinforce the commitment to tackling cyberbullying in their communities.

Notes

1. M. O'Moore, 'Cyberbullying: The Situation in Ireland', *Pastoral Care in Education* 30 (2012): pp. 209–23.
2. Department of Education and Skills, *Anti-Bullying Procedures for Primary and Post-Primary Schools* (2013).
3. S. Livingstone, K. Ólafsson, B. O'Neill and V. Donosa, *Towards a Better Internet For Children*, www.eukidsonline.net (2012).
4. Pupil, aged sixteen. O'Moore (2012), op. cit.
5. O'Moore (2012), op. cit.
6. M. Lawlor, P. Courtney, A. Flynn, B. Henry and N. Murphy, 'Bullying Behaviour in Secondary Schools: What Roles do Teachers Play?', *Child Abuse Review* 17 (2008): pp. 160–73.
7. E. Roland, E. Bru, U. V. Midthassel and G. S. Vaaland, *Social Psychology of Education* 3 (2010): pp. 41–55.

8. Livingstone, Ólafsson, O'Neill and Donosa (2012), op. cit.
9. L. Bond, H. Butler, L. Thomas, J. Carlin and S. Glover, 'Social and School Connectedness in Early Secondary School as Predictors of Late Teenage Substance Use, Mental Health and Academic Outcomes', *Journal of Adolescent Health* 40 (2007): pp. 357.9–357.18.
10. M. O'Moore, 'The Four Pillars of Action: The Role of Guidance Counsellors in Developing and Implementing the Whole School Community Approach in Tackling Bullying, both Traditional and Cyber', www.schoolguidancehandbook.ncge.ie/search/bully (2013).
11. The Irish Association of Suicidology, *Suicide Prevention in Schools: Best Practice Guidelines* (2000).
12. A. P. Goldstein, B. Glick and J. C. Gibbs, *Aggressive Replacement Training: A Comprehensive Intervention for Aggressive Youth* (Illinois: Research Press, 1998).
13. F. Thompson and P. K. Smith, *The Use and Effectiveness of Anti-Bullying Strategies in Schools*, research brief DFE-RB088, http://www.education.gov.uk/publications/ (2011).
14. J. Woulfe, 'Secondary School Suspends 28 Pupils for Cyberbullying on Facebook', *The Irish Times* (12 March 2013).
15. M. Dayton, 'A Review of Suspension and Expulsion as Appropriate Instrument of Sanction in Second Level Education in Ireland', unpublished PhD thesis (Trinity College, University of Dublin, 2013).
16. R. M. Kowalski, S. P. Limber and P. W. Agatston, *Cyberbullying: Bullying in the Digital Age* (London: Wiley-Blackwell, 2012).
17. Ibid.
18. O'Moore (2012), op. cit.
19. H. Thomt Ruud, '20,000 Norske barn sendte nakenbilde av seg selv', *Dagbladet* (29 April 2014), p. 16.
20. D. Strohmeier, C. Hoffmann, E. M. Schiller, E. Stefanek and C. Spiel, 'ViSC Social Competence Program', *New Directions for Youth Development* 133 (2012): pp. 71–80.
21. B. Boyd, 'Getting the Message Through that Moderation is the Norm', *The Irish Times Health and Family Supplement* (4 June 2013).
22. H. W. Perkins, D. W. Craig and J. M. Perkins, 'Using Social Norms to Reduce Bullying: A Research Intervention Among Adolescents in Five Middle Schools', *Group Processes Intergroup Relations* 14 (2011): pp. 703–22.
23. 'Let's Kick it Out Campaign', Watch Your Space, www.watchyourspace.ie/get ideas/lets-kick-it-out-campaign/ (accessed 7 July 2014).
24. Thompson and Smith (2011), op. cit.
25. Strohmeier, Hoffmann, Schiller, Stefanek and Spiel (2012), op. cit.

PART THREE

Cyberbullying and the Home

WHAT PARENTS CAN DO TO COUNTER CYBERBULLYING

There is no rowing back; the digital age is our children's future. It offers them outstanding opportunities for communication, learning and entertainment. However, it does not come without its risks. Cyberbullying has the potential, as seen in Chapter 5, to be extremely harmful to all those who are targeted, young or old, to the extent that it can change their self-belief and mood and, as a consequence, trigger depression and even suicide. Parents are in a key position to help prevent and confront cyberbullying so that neither their own children nor those of others need to suffer victimisation.

Supervision and Monitoring of Online Activities

According to Eleanor Mills, parents of school-going children and adolescents

> exist in a state of perma-anxiety about the number of square-eyed hours their children spend gawping at screens or killing aliens. Screen time – or the removal of it – is one of the biggest bazookas in today's parenting arensal: 'Tidy your bedroom or no Nintendo Wii tonight' or 'Finish your homework and you can have half an hour dressing up mannequins on Girls Go Games.'¹

There is little doubt that supervising and monitoring screen time has taken its place among the many other concerns, challenges and responsibilities of parenthood. It is understandable that many parents may feel unable to adequately supervise their children's use of the communication technologies due to their own lack of knowledge or ability to keep up with fast-evolving digital devices. However, rather than stand back and do nothing, there is much parents can learn from their children. Asking children for information can be very affirming for them, strengthening their sense of self-worth. It can also provide the perfect opportunity to gain an understanding of the level of their internet safety skills. The more expert they are, the more you can be reassured that they will not be so easily taken advantage of when online.

Every day, children and adolescents across the globe go online and make decisions that can compromise their safety, security and privacy. They can chat with each other, listen to music, view videos, go shopping and find information to almost all of their queries. In Ireland, half of all nine- to sixteen-year-olds have been found to use the internet on a daily basis with this rising to three-quarters of all adolescents.[2] In Norway – a country approximately the same size as Ireland – 20,000 children (thirteen to sixteen) have sent naked pictures of themselves via their smartphones or computers.[3] No doubt in years to come, as wireless networks and smartphones become ever more commonplace, it will be the exceptional child or adolescent who will not have the opportunity or the desire to go online.

Even though the internet is rich in safety information and resources, many children have been groomed, cajoled or forced to take intimate pictures of themselves. As reported in Part One, the more frequent the use of the internet, the greater the risk of becoming a victim and a cyberbully.[4] Preventing cyberbullying requires that children know how to stay safe when communicating online. Children as young as five are members of virtual worlds such as Moshi Monsters and Club Penguin, and it has been noted that young children become more distressed when things go wrong; for example, when they are socially excluded from games by friends, when friends and siblings misuse their online profiles and when they encounter virtual losses (games being hijacked or ruined, or losing virtual currency).

The first step for parents in safeguarding their children from being cyberbullied is to determine their child's level of understanding of the risks involved when they are accessing the internet. The knowledge they possess should guide the level of filtering software, supervision and monitoring that may be required to keep them safe from inappropriate content and undesirable online friendships.

As yet we do not have the evidence that children under nine have the capacity to stay safe online, especially when it comes to social-networking sites. Although sites such as YouTube, Facebook, Flickr and Twitter stipulate that members must be thirteen or older, there is evidence to show that close to 40% of eleven- to twelve-year-olds have a social networking profile despite the age restriction. It has also been shown that 80% of children under thirteen years of age who have an account on a social-networking site received help to set one up from their parents (33% from a father; 30% from a mother), siblings (17%) and friends (30%).[5]

It is noteworthy that online monitoring by parents of the underage users has been found to be less than that of the older children. Contributing to the lack of monitoring may be that younger children's online activities are considered pretty harmless, such as playing games and chatting to friends, in comparison to older children's online activities. However, it may also be that parents are uncomfortable supervising and monitoring as they have colluded in helping their child falsify their birth date. Whatever the reasons may be, it is a cause of concern as Swedish researchers have found that 13% of parents of three- to seven-year-olds and 20% of parents of eight- to eleven-year-olds have reported that their child has had a negative experience online.[6]

As children grow older they are increasingly exposed to online risks. Over one-third of Irish girls, for example, have been subjected to some form of harmful content, such as hate messages (15%), anorexic (pro-ana) or bulimic content (14%), self-harm sites (9%), sites discussing suicide (8%) and sites where people share their experiences of drugs (7%). Also, nearly half (47%) of older adolescents have seen sexual images, and one in ten thirteen- to fourteen-year-olds and over one in five fifteen- to sixteen-year-olds have received sexual messages online. Furthermore, and of considerable concern, is the finding that one in five have had contact with people they have never met face to face.[7]

Despite having an understanding of the risks online, children, especially younger ones, are still vulnerable to internet use. For example, although five- to eight-year-olds were able to identify content risks (sexual content, violence and inappropriate language, or risks regarding meeting people they only knew online), they displayed a degree of naivety when they were shown real-life internet scenarios. They were, for example, unable to identify inappropriate communication, commercialism, unreliable information and revealing personal information as risks. When asked if they would go to a birthday party or to the park for a game after being invited by a person they only knew on the internet, some said 'yes'.[8]

125

The conclusion to be drawn from these findings is that parents need to be aware that young children's knowledge about internet risks may not always translate into safe behaviours during internet encounters. Parents must stay vigilant of their young children's online behaviour. Also, to reduce unnecessary risks regarding online contact and material, parents should install filtering software to prevent upsetting and inappropriate content when children navigate the web.

Striking a Balance Between Monitoring and Digital Literacy

Family safety settings in Microsoft Windows 8 and parental controls in Windows 7 and Windows Vista help to create a safer online environment for children by allowing parents to track and monitor their online activities. Blocking or allowing access to selected websites and choosing which games or apps children can access is also possible. However, no amount of software will be foolproof in avoiding hateful or sexual content.

It is well known that children and adolescents – especially those who enjoy risk-taking behaviours – often access the internet using smartphones or computers outside the home. A recent study confirmed that ownership numbers and use of smartphones, laptops or tablets by nine- to sixteen-year-olds did not necessarily match. Indeed, nearly half (47%) admitted to accessing the internet in their friends' or relatives' homes, libraries and cafes, with over one-third doing so every week.[9] Also, many technologically sophisticated children can get around the filtering and blocking software put in place by parents. So the solution to protecting children from harmful material and contacts is to strike a balance between monitoring and digital literacy.

Talk to Children About Safe Use

With the help of the American Academy of Pediatrics (AAP), Microsoft Security have developed detailed age-based guidelines for internet use.[10] The younger the child, the greater the need for supervision and for clear rules about internet use.

The Anti-Bullying Centre (ABC) 'Tips for Staying Cyber-Safe' are as follows:

Social Networking

- Do not accept 'friend invites' from people you do not know; exercise the same caution you would with a stranger you meet on the street.
- Make sure your privacy settings are set so that only your friends can view your personal information and photos. If your profile is set to 'public' anybody can view your photos and anything you or your friends write online.
- Be sensible about what personal information you include in your profile. Keep it general and exercise great caution in listing details of your home address, mobile number, email address, and the school or sports club you attend.
- Do not assume just because your profile is 'private' that your conversations are too. If someone hacks into your friend's profile, then they will also be able to view all your information.
- Make it a rule of thumb not to divulge anything online that you would not be happy to say out loud in a crowded room.
- Disable 'anonymous' questions in the settings on Ask.fm.
- Learn how to 'block' and 'report' other profiles on sites like Facebook and Twitter."

It is often recommended that internet-connected computers should be kept in an open area, where they can easily be supervised. However, as households are increasingly wireless and smartphones, laptops and tablets are becoming more commonplace, it is unrealistic to insist on children engaging in online activities in an open area. One way to overcome the potential problems of allowing children connect to the internet in their bedrooms is to sign up to a parental control system, such as that offered by Norton 360. This will allow you to know which websites and social networks your child visits and what they search for.

However, most beneficial is building trust and encouraging non-judgemental open dialogue with children. Adolescents in particular can become defensive and irritated when they are made to feel that they cannot manage their own affairs – it strips them of their confidence, making them feel inferior and dependent. Children thrive when they are given the freedom to discover things for themselves and to overcome obstacles. They tend to confide in their parents more when they feel valued and listened to and receive feedback which is non-judgemental and positive.

With this in mind, parents should try to strike a balance between caution and anxiety about digital risks. There is no better way to achieve this than to have a conversation about internet safety and responsible behaviour (digital citizenship) with your child. It is vital that they understand that true anonymity in cyberspace is an illusion. Digital footprints can be traced even if a person uses a name other than their own. It is important that children understand that their digital footprint can impact on their future reputation and employment prospects.

Talking to Children About Cyberbullying

Parents should take the precaution of talking to children about cyberbullying and not wait until it happens. They should emphasise that it is not uncommon for children to feel shame or to blame themselves when they are victims of cyberbullying, and explain that they understand why the child may be reluctant to share their problem. However, it is important to let children know that should they find themselves subjected to cyberbullying, no one will think worse of them or deny them their phone or online access, but that they will get help to resolve the situation. It is recommended that parents become familiar with their children's school policy and procedures for reporting and investigating allegations of cyberbullying.

The following tips can be given to children in the event of cyberbullying:

If you are being targeted by cyberbullies
- Don't feel ashamed: The shame lies with the perpetrator. Remember it's not about you. Often people who bully others do so to make themselves feel better because they are unhappy. Do not blame yourself, it is not your fault.
- Don't reply to abusive or hurtful messages: Do not respond to unwanted texts, instead turn off your phone for a few days or change your number. If you are receiving unwanted calls, do not hang up straight away as this may feed the caller's wish to scare you, instead walk away and hang up a few minutes later.

- Save the message: Do not delete the offensive text, email, phone call, video clip or image, this should instead be kept as evidence.
- Think about purchasing an application that would allow you to control who calls or sends you texts, such as Bully Stop at www.vmad.com.
- Block the sender.
- Do not ignore the bullying: Tell someone you trust. Report the threatening or offensive behaviour to your parent or teacher and/ or contact the service provider (through its Customer Care or Report Abuse facility). Share evidence of cyberbullying with the school. Most often the boys and girls who cyberbully also engage in traditional face-to-face bullying, so it is important that the school gets to know about it so that they can apprehend the perpetrators. With cyberbullying, you have the advantage of being able to show copies of the offensive messages, pictures or video clips.
- If the cyberbullying is very threatening and serious contact your local Gardaí.[12]

In view of the considerable overlap between cyber and traditional victimisation, it is critical that children are also aware of what to do if they are subjected to bullying offline. The following guidelines may be helpful:

If you are being targeted by bullies
- Remember it's not about you: That may sometimes feel hard to believe, but it's true. Often people who bully others do it to make themselves feel better because they are unhappy at school or at home. Remember that *they* have the problem, not you. Don't believe what they say to you, and don't blame yourself.
- What to do? Act as confident as you can. Face them and tell them clearly to stop. Try and be calm and move away from them. Telling them clearly and publically to stop means they cannot say later that it was 'only a joke' or they didn't know you were unhappy.
- Do *not* hit out! If someone is bullying you, don't try to hit or kick them. You may get hurt in a fight and even if you don't, the bully can sometimes use how you hit them against you, and make it seem like *you* are the bully. You may have no choice but to defend

yourself if they are physically attacking but even then do your best to walk away, as getting into a fight can be used against you.

- If they call you names: It can be hard but if they tease you or slag you off, try and laugh it off. Don't let them see that they have hurt you. Bullies like to get a reaction, they thrive on it, and if they don't get one there is no point in bullying you.
- Tell your friends/people you trust in class: Tell them what is going on and how you feel. Ask them to witness what is going on (especially if people are making gestures or other actions that teachers may not see). Ask them to come with you to tell a teacher if you are afraid. Ask them to stand up for you against the bully. There is safety in numbers, and the more voices raised the more notice will be taken.
- Tell someone! If you're being bullied, try and tell someone about it, be it your parents, someone in your family, your teachers or a helpline.
- What to say when you tell: Tell them what has happened, who is doing it, how often it has happened, if anyone saw or heard what went on, and what you have tried to do about it.
- If your school has a peer support or mentoring programme try to use it: No one can help you if you don't tell them. If you are afraid to tell because it might make things worse, tell the person you talk to that this is what you're afraid of, and ask them to find a way to help you deal with it so it won't.[13]

In addition to making clear where they stand in relation to the prevention and intervention of cyber-victimisation, parents need to be equally explicit in letting children know that the cyberbullying of others is strongly disapproved of. Indeed, children should be made aware that by cyberbullying others they are saying more about themselves than their victims and laying bare their own inadequacies and weaknesses. Furthermore, in expressing disapproval of cyberbullying, it is important to discuss the problem of being both a bully and a victim. To be forewarned is to be forearmed, and it is as well for children to know that they can confide in their parents even if they have reacted to their victimisation by bullying their aggressors.

It is also important to take the time to encourage children to intervene when they are witnesses to cyberbullying. If every parent reinforced positive bystander behaviour it would probably be the most effective way to counteract all forms of bullying. And, as a result, parents would have peace in the knowledge that their child would be protected by their peers.

Talking About Coping Strategies

Chapter 6 described the different coping strategies children and adolescents commonly use when they feel they are being cyberbullied, and discussed the tendency of children and adolescents to use ineffective coping strategies. The most effective strategies are to seek support and to take an assertive stance. It is destructive for mental health to take a passive approach or to retaliate in a reactive aggressive manner.

Most importantly, children need to know that direct requests for help are very effective in getting bystanders to take action. It is recommended, therefore, that when parents discuss cyberbullying with their children, they make reference to the scientific findings in Chapter 6. This will help them to cope better should they experience a cyber-attack.

The advice for children should be:

- Do not to respond to a cyberbullying incident in an insulting, threatening or aggressive manner
- Warn those who cyberbully to stop, otherwise you will report them
- If identity is known, a warning can also be given face to face
- Seek support and ask for help from friends, family and teachers.

Important as the above tips are for any child, they will sit more easily with a child or teenager who is confident and assertive in social situations and who is also resilient, empathic and has an ability to resolve conflicts and manage anger well. Should you recognise that a child is lacking in any of these skills, efforts should be made to boost them. Parents can develop these attributes in their children. However, professional help can correct any specific social skills which you feel may be lacking and which you feel may be holding a child back from enjoying good peer status and support. With assistance from school guidance counsellors or an external professional, social and emotional deficiencies can be corrected.

Reducing the Digital Divide Between Parents and Children

It is not uncommon for children, teenagers in particular, to be more technologically advanced than their parents. Adults generally regard computers as practical tools, whereas for children the internet is a lifeline to their peers, serving, in the words of one of my sons, as 'another playground'. We hear of children, for example, who have multiple Facebook accounts, one for their parents to see and others that give them freedom from parental interference. Furthermore, the more parents embrace sites like Facebook, the more children are prompted to seek other sites to avoid scrutiny. These sites often only come to adults' full attention when there has been a news story associated with their use, such as the suicide linked with Ask.fm in 2012.[14]

Staying reasonably up to date with children's understanding of technology requires that parents take advantage of that knowledge and ask their children to explain what they do online. In addition, parents should attend any awareness-raising courses that may be held either in school or as part of evening courses in the local community. There are also some good self-help books and websites for this purpose. The Department of Justice and Equality's Office for Internet Safety has developed excellent guides for parents in print or electronic form, including the *Get With It!* series. These guides deal with new media technologies, filtering technologies and social-networking sites. Their content invites parents to discuss concerns they may have about their child's online activities, and to assess whether or not their children have the skills to avoid cyberbullying.

Netiquette

Cyberbullying can be prevented if a child appreciates that internet safety is not just about technical skills, but about knowing how to conduct themselves online. Having good manners online is commonly referred to as 'netiquette' (online etiquette) or digital citizenship.

Virginia Shea's core rules of netiquette are:

- Remember the human (at the other end of the electronic communication is a person with feelings that can be hurt)
- Adhere to the same standards of behaviour online that you follow in real life (never send something you would not say to a person face to face)
- Know where you are in cyberspace (standards of netiquette can vary)
- Respect other people's time and bandwidth (what is important to you may not be so for others)
- Make yourself look good online (make sense, don't use flame bait)
- Share expert knowledge (share information if asked on discussion groups)
- Help keep flame wars under control (don't respond to flame mail);
- Respect other people's privacy (don't read other people's private communications)
- Don't abuse your power (if you have power use it well)
- Be forgiving of other people's mistakes (don't forget you were also once a digital newcomer).[15]

Saving the Evidence

When children receive a horrible image or message, the temptation is to delete it. However, having hard evidence of the cyberbullying behaviour will strengthen the case and make the investigations easier should it go as far as police intervention. Thus, a precautionary measure is to let children know the importance of saving any nasty and upsetting material directed at them (this involves making sure they know how to do screen grabs). If the messages are anonymous, they should be saved to the computer's hard drive and then forwarded, if appropriate, to the school or internet service provider. If the cyberbullying is very threatening and disturbing it should be passed to the Gardaí in order for them to trace the perpetrator.

Talk to Children About the Legal Consequences of Cyberbullying

The more knowledgeable children are about the legal consequences of cyberbullying, the less likely they are to become involved in such behaviour. (Refer to 'Some Law on Cyberbullying', page 165, to see what the law at present says about the common behaviours connected to cyberbullying.)

Encourage Positive Bystanding

There is little doubt that children know better than the rest of us about the high cost of cyberbullying. Yet, in spite of their power to lessen the impact, it is the minority who admit to helping their peers when they are cyberbullied. In recognition of the importance of peer support in stopping bullying in all its forms, most school anti-bullying programmes address this topic with their pupils. However, it is important that every parent strengthens the school's message.

Children, like adults, are fearful of supporting a person in difficulty due to a lack of confidence in their ability to intervene effectively. There is also the fear of negative consequences, such as becoming the next victim. In addition, the strength of the bystander's social conscience plays a part. (See Chapter 6 for a fuller discussion of these factors.) However, we regularly hear about people being rewarded for acts of bravery – acts carried out more from a sense of civic responsibility, not as a result of having the necessary skills. Every opportunity should therefore be taken at home to encourage and to reinforce effective coping skills, as well as making children feel that they have a responsibility to help their peers.

Being a positive bystander does not mean that your child must intervene at the moment of witness, but rather that they should find an opportunity to support the victim in private. Reaching out a hand of friendship will always be remembered. They can also let a staff member know so that they can stop the perpetrator(s) and provide any professional support that is needed for the victim.

If a child is not fearful of reprisal, an effective way to stop bullying is to take the bully aside and let them know that they will report them unless they stop. Gathering friends to confront the bully is likely to add strength to such a warning. Being a defender, especially when confronting the bully, is made easier if a child is empathic and has sturdy self-esteem.

Much can be achieved by having a conversation with children about active citizenship and encouraging them not to turn a blind eye to hurtful behaviour. By not intervening they should understand that their behaviour will be interpreted as showing approval and support for the perpetrators. On the other hand, by intervening they are helping to reduce the level of bullying in their school.

Below are some tips to empower children to take action against cyberbullying:

- Share 'bystander' feelings of upset, fear or anger with friends, family and staff members
- Never be manipulated into thinking the victim deserves to be tormented or made fun of
- Never encourage the perpetrators by forwarding hurtful messages or images that are shared by the perpetrator
- Encourage friends to send the perpetrator(s) the message that 'this is not on'
- Let the victim know that they do not have to put up with it and that they must report it and offer to help if necessary.

Chapter 9: Key Messages
- Talking to children about cyberbullying is key to prevention. Make sure they understand why it is wrong to use cyberbully tactics or to assist or reinforce a classmate or friend who might be cyberbullying.
- Make sure children understand the need to stay safe when online and that they have the skills to do so.
- Reduce the digital divide between adult and child as much as possible with the help of the child's own knowledge, self-help materials or courses.
- Set rules or a code of behaviour for safe internet use within the family.
- Strike a balance between supervising and monitoring online activities and trusting children to avoid risky online behaviour.
- Talk to children about the possible coping strategies to deal with cyberbullying.
- Talk to children about the legal implications of cyberbullying and harassment.
- Become aware of the importance of good social skills in preventing cyberbullying, and strengthen any deficiencies that you feel may put a child at risk of becoming involved as a victim, bully or both.

- Impress upon children that they can help reduce the level of bullying and cyberbullying in their school and society by taking positive action to stop the bullying or to report it.

Notes

1. M. Eleanor, 'Being a Luddite is not Pukka, Jamie', *Sunday Times* (3 November 2013).
2. B. O'Neill, S. Grehan and K. Ólafson, *Risks and Safety for Children on the Internet: The Ireland Report* (London: LSE, 2011).
3. H. Thomt Ruud, '20,000 Norske barn sendte nakenbilde av seg selv', *Dagbladet* (29 April 2014), p. 16.
4. T. Heiman and D. Olenik Shemesh, 'Youth Cyberbullying: Risk, Intervention and Prevention', *Advances in Psychology Research* 96 (2013): pp. 1–17.
5. D. Holloway, L. Green and S. Livingstone, *Zero to Eight: Young Children and Their Internet Use* (London: LSE, 2013).
6. O. Findahl, *Swedes and the Internet 2012*. Retrieved from https://www.iis.se/docs/Swedes-and-the-Internet-2012.pdf (2012) (accessed 1 September 2014).
7. B. O'Neill and T. Dinh, *Net Children Go Mobile: Initial Findings from Ireland* (Dublin: Dublin Institute of Technology, 2014).
8. L. A. Ey and C. G. Cupit, 'Exploring Young Children's Understanding of Risks Associated with Internet Usage and Their Concepts of Management Strategies', *Journal of Early Childhood Research* 9 (2011): pp. 53–6.
9. O'Neill and Dinh (2014), op. cit.
10. Microsoft Security, Age-Based Guidelines for Kids' Internet Use, http://www.microsoft.com/security/family-safety/childsafety-age.aspx.
11. Anti-Bullying Centre, Dublin City University, http://www4.dcu.ie/abc/.
12. Ibid.
13. Ibid.
14. 'The Tragedy of Bullying', *The Irish Times* (1 November 2012).
15. V. Shea, *Netiquette* (San Francisco: Albion Books, 1994).

STEPS TO TAKE IF YOUR CHILD IS BEING CYBERBULLIED

The media attention given to cyberbullying's association with suicide has understandably struck fear into the hearts of many parents. It is understandable, therefore, that emotions are likely to run high when parents either suspect or gain evidence that their child is being cyberbullied. There may even be feelings of guilt and self-blame at not having recognised or reacted sooner to tell-tale signs of victimisation.

As with traditional bullying, it can be extremely difficult for a parent to know for certain if their child is being cyberbullied, due to the extreme reluctance of children to let parents know. But should you suspect that your child is a victim of cyberbullying due to changes in their social relationships (e.g. reluctance to go to school or engage in after-school activities) and mood (e.g. being emotional when on the phone or online, or after receiving a call, text or logging off), it is time to take action.

In view of the strong relationship between bullying, depressive mood and thoughts of suicide, it is important for parents to be aware of the most common clinical manifestations of depression. It is important to note that symptoms vary with age. Messina and Tiedemann note that in preschool children (up to age six or seven) the most common clinical manifestations are physical symptoms such as pains (principally head and abdomen) and fatigue and dizziness.[1] They add that in this period suicidal thoughts or attempts do not occur. However, children who do not verbalise their emotions may show self-destructive behaviour in the form of repeated head bashing, biting oneself or swallowing dangerous objects.

Whereas school-age children tend to communicate their depressed mood with sadness, irritability or boredom, depressed adolescents are not always sad. They are primarily irritated and unstable, and can have emotional outbursts and anger. Alcohol and drug use can also characterise depression in adolescents.

While it may be tempting to think that the association between bullying and suicide ideation is exaggerated, there is strong scientific evidence to indicate that the risk of suicidal ideation is 2.4 times greater among youth who experience peer victimisation in the previous year.[2]

Depression symptoms in school-age children and adolescents

School-age Children (six to twelve years)	Adolescents (from twelve years)
1. Sadness, irritability and/or dullness 2. Lack of ability to enjoy themselves 3. Sad appearance 4. Crying easily 5. Fatigue 6. Isolation and weak relationship with peers 7. Low self-esteem 8. Diminished or weak school performance 9. Separation anxiety 10. Phobias 11. Death desire or ideation 12. Suicidal ideas and attempts 13. Severe behavioural problems	1. Irritability and instability 2. Depressed humour 3. Loss of energy 4. Lack of motivation and significant lack of interest 5. Psychomotor retardation 6. Feelings of hopelessness and/or guilt 7. Sleep disorders 8. Isolation 9. Difficulty concentrating 10. Poor school performance 11. Low self-esteem

In a similar manner to dealing with traditional bullying, start with gently trying to get your child to open up and unburden themselves to you. You can begin by saying, 'I have noticed you haven't been yourself recently. I can't help wondering if someone is giving you a hard time.' Explain to your child that cyberbullying is becoming more commonplace but that no one deserves to be bullied in this way or in any other way. Explain also that whatever they may perceive to be the cause of the cyberbullying, they should not blame themselves, as any feelings of shame rightly belong to the perpetrators. Importantly, let your child know that even if they have done something to provoke the cyberbullying, it is better to discuss it at home to see how it can best be resolved. Reassure them that you will not judge them or think less of them, but you want to help them find a way to stop the bullying. It is important to let them know that you will not do anything that may cause reprisals or risk an escalation of the cyberbullying. Whichever way you approach the subject, it is important that your child gets the message that being a cyber-victim can happen to the best of people and getting help has been shown to be the most effective way to both lessen the emotional impact and to stop it.

Should there be no sign of improvement in mood and you have gained no hard evidence to support your suspicions, you have two main choices. One is to talk to parents of your child's good friends and ask them if they will gently probe their children for clues. The other is to approach the school to see if they have observed any change in behaviour, and if so what thoughts they might have by way of an explanation. If appropriate, suggest that the school guidance counsellor or your GP has a word with your child to tease out what may lie at the root of the change in mood. This may give you the information you need to either allay your fears or to continue to seek answers to your concerns. It is vital that you let your child know that you are concerned about the changes in their behaviour and to stress that a problem shared is a problem halved.

Making Contact with the School

Should you choose to make contact with the school, you need to follow the procedures developed for reporting incidents of bullying in their anti-bullying policy. When speaking with the relevant staff member, it would be helpful if you have some evidence of the cyberbullying, such as copies of emails, text messages and instant message conversations. If the cyber-material is anonymous ask the school to help you trace the perpetrator. Apart from using technology to trace the perpetrators, they can talk to peers and to teachers. It is not uncommon for the identity of the perpetrators to become known through conversation with the peer group. Finding out who sent the messages or images may help to alleviate the anxiety caused by the anonymous cyber-attacks. However, the disciplinary action as outlined in the school's anti-bullying policy should be followed.

Contacting Parents of Alleged Perpetrators

Contacting parents or carers of alleged perpetrators of cyberbullying should only be an option if the children do not go to the same school. If they do, contacting the parents should be delayed until attempts by the school have proved unsuccessful in stopping the cyberbullying.

While there is a strong likelihood that parents of traditional bullying victims will be met with a defensive manner (reinforcing the view that bullying behaviour in children has its roots in the parental behaviour), with cyberbullying, if parents are approached in a calm and sensitive manner, the response has proven to be more positive.[3] One reason is that it becomes more difficult for parents of alleged cyberbullies to deny their child's involvement when there is evidence at hand. Another contributing factor may be that the parents of the alleged cyberbully also learn that their son or daughter may also be a victim. Chapter 4 outlined the extent to which children who cyberbully are also victims of both cyber and traditional bullying. When parents learn that their child's inappropriate online behaviour may be reactive rather than premeditated, the chances are that they will be more amenable to resolving the problem.

Should parents of the perpetrator(s) not respond in a helpful manner, you should outline to them your next steps, such as contacting the alleged cyberbully's school. If the cyberbullying is of a serious nature you have the option of letting them know that you may contact your solicitor and/or the Gardaí, who may notify them of the possible legal consequences should the cyberbullying continue or should the offensive material not be removed.

Legal Options

It is recommended that the Gardaí are notified of cyberbullying if it is anonymous and of a serious nature. For legal action to be considered it is usual that cyberbullying includes:

- Threats of physical harm
- Defamatory material
- Incitement to hatred
- Harassment and stalking
- Extortion.

140

Critically, legal action should only be a first step if you are confident that the bullying is not carried out by a member of your child's school. Otherwise it would be preferable to contact your school first and let them decide whether legal action needs to be taken.

Dealing with a Cyberbullying Victim

If your child or teenager has been cyberbullied, and maybe also traditionally bullied, it is likely that it will have taken its toll on their sense of self, their confidence and their joy of life. It is the damage to the sense of self that can be a source of much psychological pain and can be a source of depression and thoughts of suicide.

The greater the resilience and self-esteem your child has, the better they will be able to withstand the impact of the bullying. However, if you feel that your child has suffered emotionally due to cyberbullying, it is vital that you give them plenty of quality time and affirmation at every opportunity. Make sure that the other members of the family also behave positively towards them. Stress that the problem lies with the cyberbully and that you and your family will help them cope with the bullying and the emotional distress. This may mean going through the Anti-Bullying Centre's 'Tips for Staying Cyber-Safe' to avoid any risky internet behaviour that may have triggered the bullying and the 'If you are being targeted by cyberbullies/bullies' advice and coping strategies, all outlined in Chapter 9. It may also mean taking steps to rebuild self-esteem, develop greater assertiveness skills and resilience as well as alleviating any social or emotional anxiety, symptoms of depression and thoughts of suicide that may have been caused by the bullying.

Should your child suffer the self-blame that often accompanies bullying, it is vital that you help them realise that they are not to blame. It has been found that once victims become convinced they are not at fault, it repairs the psychological damage caused by the cyberbullying.[4] However, should you sense that your child is suffering from depression, do not hesitate to seek immediate professional advice. It is important that children learn that there are other ways to ease the psychological pain than through self-harm and suicide, which continues to be a risk of cyberbullying, especially if combined with traditional bullying.

Chapter 10: Key Messages

- To be a victim of cyberbullying can cause great upset, with associated behavioural and performance-related changes.
- The reluctance of victims to let parents and teachers know makes it very difficult to be confident that any behavioural changes relate to cyberbullying.
- If you are worried, talk to parents of your son or daughter's friends or the school to see if they can provide a reason why your child or teenager is out of sorts.
- Contacting parents of the perpetrator(s) should only be an option if those involved in cyberbullying do not go to the same school.
- Contact the Gardaí if the cyberbullying poses a serious threat to your child's health and safety.
- Keep copies and a record of all cyberbullying activities.
- Deal with any psychosomatic, emotional and behavioural changes that may have arisen as a result of the cyberbullying. Do not be critical or dismiss children's feelings. Give them extra time and unconditional love. Emphasise that they should not blame themselves, as it is the bully who has the problem.
- If you note symptoms of depression and thoughts of suicide, seek immediate professional help and keep the school informed of the therapeutic treatment that your child is receiving. This will allow the staff to be sensitive to the psychological pain that your child may be experiencing.

Notes

1. L. F. Messina and K. B. Tiedemann, 'Psychobiological Depression in Childhood and Adolescence: A Clinical Review' (2006), http://www.priory.com/psych/childdepreview.htm (accessed 7 July 2014).
2. H. A. Turner, D. Finkelhor, A. Shattuck and S. Hamby, 'Recent Victimization Exposure and Suicidal Ideation in Adolescents', *Archives of Pediatrics & Adolescent Medicine* 166 (2012): pp. 1149–54.
3. R. M. Kowalski, S. P. Limber and P. W. Agatston, *Cyberbullying: Bullying in the Digital Age* (London: Wiley-Blackwell, 2012).
4. Cited in S. and P. Fried, *Bullies and Victims: Helping Your Child Through the Schoolyard Battlefield* (New York: M. Evans and Company, 1996).

STEPS TO TAKE IF YOUR CHILD IS CYBERBULLYING OTHERS

No parent is happy to learn that their child has been involved in cyberbullying, either as the ringleader or as a hanger-on. We are all aware that, to a large extent, our children's behaviour mirrors our own behaviour, attitudes and values. Thus, by behaving inappropriately they prompt us to ask ourselves what is it about our parenting that may be contributing to the negative behaviours. Yet it is never too late to correct inappropriate behaviours that may reflect some weakness in our patterns of child-rearing. There is good guidance to be gained from self-help books and parenting courses, and from trained professionals who can work with parents and children to help with difficulties that may be holding children back from enjoying good peer relationships.

Childhood and adolescence is a time of learning, and that includes absorbing the duties and responsibilities that come with being a member of a community. No parent serves their child well by overlooking their behaviour when they see or hear that they have been heavy-handed in their dealings with others. There is increasing evidence from longitudinal studies (see Chapter 4) of the poor outcomes in adulthood of children whose bullying behaviour has not been corrected. While most of these studies are based on traditional bullying, there is no reason to doubt that the outcomes will be any different for cyberbullying as there is little to distinguish cyberbullies from traditional bullies.

The warning signs that a child has a propensity to cyberbully others can be the same as those of traditional bullying. Specific to cyberbullying, however, are the following signs:

- Easily threatened, quick to get into an argument or fight with siblings and peers, and quick to blame others
- Often teases or uses put downs when referring to peers
- Regards cyberbullying as a bit of fun and can't understand the big fuss that is made about it
- Spends a lot of time on the internet

- Very defensive or secretive about online activities. May react with anger when a parent enters the room or may close down the webpage or computer
- Showing extremes of emotion – from hilarity to hostility – when online, either alone or with a group of friends.

As with traditional bullying it is vital that cyberbullying is nipped in the bud. As a parent, this means not only challenging any cyberbullying behaviour that comes to one's attention, but responding positively to complaints of alleged bullying from teachers, other parents or indeed the Gardaí.

Learning that your child has been involved in cyberbullying should not be met with a punitive response, as bullying is frequently transient and is an expression of some form of stress, feelings of unhappiness, worthlessness, frustration, perceived lack of love and unmet needs of attention and recognition. Identifying and attending to the causative factors as soon as possible will help to correct underlying causes and thus prevent further bullying behaviours.

Reasons and triggers can be many, and some may have their roots in exposure to aggressive behaviour in the home. Such behaviour is often an expression of poorly developed social skills and, in particular, a lack of emotional empathy. In correcting negative behaviour it is important not to discourage your child but to express all feedback in a positive manner. For example, rather than saying 'You can't just fire off a message without thinking about the effects', it is preferable to say something along the lines of 'Remember to always think before you decide to send a message or image to someone'.

Steps for Dealing with a Child Who is Cyberbullying
Coping with a child or teenager who cyberbullies is not dissimilar to the strategies you would use for dealing with a traditional bully, for which it is recommended that parents:

- Identify any unmet emotional needs that their child may have
- Look to their child's social skills
- Give their child something to excel in
- Look to their child's ability to manage anger

- Look to their child's sense of values and moral reasoning
- Teach respect for diversity
- Use screen violence positively. Take time to discuss the screen characters and the rights and wrongs of violence.

Regarding cyberbullying, the following strategies are vital:

- Create an accurate awareness of what cyberbullying is
- Find out what is causing the cyberbullying behaviour
- Discuss the rules for responsible internet and computer use
- Monitor and supervise internet use appropriately
- Teach skills of empathy at home
- Build self-esteem at home
- Facilitate energetic children's catharis (letting off steam in a positive way).[1]

Identifying the Motives for Cyberbullying

Discovering what causes your child to cyberbully is key to finding the most effective means to putting a stop to the behaviour. The reasons for cyberbullying can be many and varied, as shown in Chapter 4.

Should you find that your child was an inadvertent cyberbully – that they were unthinking and that the incident served as a valve for some pent-up aggression – it would probably be sufficient to talk through the principles of ethical online behaviour (netiquette) and see that they are fully understood. Communicating online can so easily be misunderstood, as there is no way of showing facial expressions or body language. Thus, a restorative approach should be tried initially. It will help your child to become more thoughtful, to take responsibility for their inappropriate behaviour and, importantly, to make amends to the victim. Your child will learn to take responsibility for their actions and will recognise that there are consequences for engaging in cyberbullying.

It is the minority of children, however, who engage exclusively in cyberbullying. And when cyber and traditional forms of bullying are combined, instrumental motives are stronger. Children are predominantly motivated by anger and sometimes fun (these motives are greater for boys than for girls). They can also be motivated by the need for friendship (affiliation) and power, but these motives are much weaker.

About half of children who display bullying behaviour have been shown to be both 'reactive' and 'instrumental' in their aggression. Only about one-third have been found to be reactively aggressive, and the minority of children (about 15%) have been shown to be instrumentally aggressive, with boys scoring higher in both forms of aggression than girls.[2] Reactive aggression is most often an angry response to some perceived provocation, threat or frustration, whereas instrumental aggression is more calculated and is often used for the purpose of demonstrating power or seeking recognition or acceptance. Other unmet needs, such as jealousy and boredom, may also be underlying motives.

Thus, whether your child is involved in cyberbullying either exclusively as a bully (pure bully) or as both a bully and a victim (bully-victim) it is most probable that both forms of aggressive behaviour have been displayed. However, should you discover that your child has combined cyber with traditional forms of bullying then their level of reactive and instrumental aggression are likely be higher than if they only cyberbullied.

Dealing with Anger

Anger is an emotional state that varies in intensity from mild irritation to intense fury and rage. Like other emotions it gives rise to physiological and biological changes, such as heart rate, blood pressure and energy hormones which regulate the fight or flight response. Both external and internal events can give rise to anger. Your child could become angry at a specific person or event (e.g. not being selected for a team) or their anger could be caused by worrying or brooding about their personal problems (e.g. poor academic achievement, lack of friendship). Memories of traumatic or maddening events can also trigger angry feelings (e.g. blamed and punished although innocent of offence). In essence, any person or event that threatens a person's pride and self-respect can give rise to anger.

The instinctive way to express anger is to respond aggressively. However, as pointed out by the American Psychological Association, laws, social norms and common sense place limits on how far anger can take us.[3] Therefore, it is critical that children learn to express their anger in an appropriate manner that does not cause harm to others.

Expressing Anger

There are three main ways of dealing with angry feelings: expressing, suppressing and calming. The healthiest way is to express anger in an assertive manner. To do this, children have to learn how to make clear what their needs are and how to get them met without hurting others. Being assertive means communicating in a respectful manner, whether off- or online.

Suppressing anger is when we hold onto the anger but stop thinking about it and focus on something else. However, if we are unsuccessful in this it can lead to passive aggressive behaviour as we turn our anger inward. Instead of face-to-face confrontations, we will get back at the person(s) indirectly. Indirect forms of traditional bullying (e.g. spreading rumours, exclusion) and cyberbullying (e.g. trolling, anonymous hate mail) lend themselves well to suppressed anger. Turning anger in on ourselves can also lead to behaviour that is both cynical and hostile. According to the American Psychological Association, 'people who are constantly putting others down, criticising everything and making cynical comments haven't learned how to constructively express their anger. Not surprisingly they aren't likely to have many successful relationships.'[4]

Calming the anger means controlling outward behaviour as well as controlling internal responses. Parents should take deliberate steps to help their children calm down until feelings of anger subside.

Anger Management

The main steps to take to help your child deal with their anger and to prevent them from being drawn to bullying as a means of expressing their anger are:

- Encourage your child to express their anger in an assertive and respectful manner. Getting angry is not going to fix anything, it generally will make matters worse. Focus instead on finding a solution
- Let your child witness assertiveness skills in the home on a daily basis. Show them that you really listen to them by repeating what they are telling you and that you understand their feelings. Suspend judgement until you have heard all sides of a story, remain calm and respond in a respectful manner. For example, learning to

use 'I' statements is the secret of good assertive communication. For example, 'I can understand how that made you angry but I am disappointed that you sent those awful messages' is preferable to reprimanding them with an angry response such as 'How could you be so mean and horrible?'

- Encourage your child to talk about the reasons for their anger. Prompt them if necessary. Is it because they are frustrated, jealous or disappointed? The more your son or daughter understands the cause of their anger, the better they will be at dealing with it
- Practise the three anger reducers: taking deep breaths, counting backwards from twenty to one and switching thoughts to a pleasant image or memory. These simple relaxation tools will help calm down angry feelings
- Encourage your child to use self-talk, i.e. telling oneself to 'cool it' or 'chill out'
- Encourage some physical or creative activity, such as drawing, model making, photography or writing
- Encourage your child to take the edge off their anger by using humour. Picture the situation or person who is the source of anger in cartoon terms. This does not mean that sarcasm is acceptable, as this is a form of unhealthy anger expression
- Give your child a hug as this can ease the tension. All too often angry and aggressive children feel unloved.[5]

As well as encouraging your child to deal with their anger in a positive and problem-solving manner, it is vital that parents model these behaviours when they experience anger. Children will get the hang of the above skills better if they are practised at home. A good way is for the family to role-play the desired strategies, with each member taking on a different role. Other than applying the above steps, consider seeking the help of professionals or professionally run courses. Mindfulness, for example, which trains us to control our thinking processes and to relax, can have beneficial effects for anger.

Dealing with False Fun
As discussed, 'fun' is a strong motive for cyberbullying. As one of the pupils in our Irish study remarked: 'People do it for fun but they

don't know how it affects people.'[6] No one would deny a child fun, but it is important that they learn that fun should never be had at the expense of other people's feelings. Furthermore, this 'false fun' may mask underlying anxiety and stress or a lack of empathy.

A lot of 'traditional' bullying is passed off by aggressors as 'only a bit of fun', or they say there were 'only joking'. But in face-to-face situations children can discern the impact of their comments or actions, and when they witness that their intended target is upset they can, if they are empathic, cease the behaviour. However, this is not possible with the majority of online communications as there are no visual cues to go by. Thus, in poking fun online children must be confident that their intended target shares their sense of humour. Naturally, mistakes are made and sometimes what was meant to be funny backfires and causes considerable offence. Such situations are usually easily remedied with an apology.

However, it is always important to uncover the underlying reason for your child poking fun at others. There might be, for example, esteem issues for which they are compensating. If cyberbullying presents itself as evidence that your child is not happy and may be trying to meet an unfulfilled need for recognition and status, then provide quality time and, if necessary, seek professional help. Dealing with insecurities as they arise will prevent compensatory behaviours from becoming habitual.

Anti-social behaviours, substance abuse and relationship issues all too often have their roots in childhood, so every effort should be taken to correct inappropriate behaviours as they arise. It is by making mistakes that we learn, so be grateful if a teacher or others point to behaviours in your child that may require attention. Studies have shown that children who were not challenged for their bullying behaviours are at an increased risk of criminal convictions, problematic relationships, domestic violence, depression and suicide in adulthood (see Chapter 5).

As a minimum intervention, it is important that you promote and reinforce the principles of netiquette and the need to value and respect others. Examples of relevant questions you might ask a child who is engaging in bullying behaviours online are:

- Would you say it to the person's face?
- What does it mean to be respectful of your classmates?
- What is the difference between 'respect' and 'like'?
- Are classmates of a different race, religion, sexuality or nationality less worthy of respect than you?

Building Empathy

If you suspect that your child is lacking in compassion then it will benefit them if you help them to build a more empathic response. Children are less inclined to bully when they recognise the ill-effects of bullying. With better emotional literacy they will be better able to understand themselves (often referred to as 'intrapersonal intelligence') and also understand others ('interpersonal intelligence'). Higher levels of intrapersonal and interpersonal intelligence sow the seeds for mutual respect and good conflict resolution skills. Thus, cyberbullying or any other form of bullying will most likely be avoided as they advance through school, further and higher education and into the workplace.

Building a greater empathic response requires that you give your child corrective feedback each time that you catch them hurting someone by words or action. Below are some tips to facilitate empathy training:

- Do not accept excuses or blame that is laid at a sibling's or a classmate's door
- Encourage your child to talk about their feelings
- Encourage your child to reflect on what triggers their emotions, on how they express the emotions and on the effects their behaviour may have on others
- Prompt your child by speculating about the motive for their cyberbullying: 'Oh, you must have felt bored or annoyed'. Whichever motive is expressed, prompt again with 'Oh, how do you think that made Jack feel?'
- Encourage your child to apologise and to make some form of amends
- Take care to model empathic behaviour in the company of your family.

Dealing with the Need for Affiliation

It is the exceptional child or teenager who does not use gaming and social-networking sites to develop and reinforce friendships. The needs of affiliation and belonging are strong motivators in human behaviour and especially so in stressful situations.[7] It concerns the wish to establish relationships and to be part of a group. Children with a strong need for affiliation will spend time creating and maintaining social relationships. They place great value on being part of a group and on being recognised, admired and accepted by all its members. It is this motive that can so often lead a child or teenager to initiate or be sucked into an anti-social act or risky behaviour, such as smoking, sexual behaviour, drug use or indeed bullying. From the time children start coming together in a play or learning environment the presence of the other children will exert an influence. However, as children become teenagers, seeking to establish an identity of their own, the peer group increasingly grows in value for them.

Each group will tend to have its own distinct identity, beliefs and values, and these will dictate the behaviour of the individual members of the group. Indeed it has been argued that the peer group exerts a greater influence than family in terms of behaviour and speech.[8] This is why it is important for parents to be aware of their child's peer group, as it will help them better understand the source of conflicts that may arise at home or at school.

Studies examining the social status of children and teenagers have found that they make up four distinct groups:

1. **Popular:** leads peers in a co-operative way, supports peers, remains calm
2. **Controversial:** leads peers, is aggressive, disruptive and controversial
3. **Rejected:** aggressive, disruptive and lacks co-operative and leadership skills
4. **Neglected:** lacks co-operative and leadership skills, not aggressive.

It is noteworthy that it is not aggression that commonly causes children to be disliked, but being disruptive, disagreeable, bossy and

151

snobbish.[9] However, it has been speculated that children who are high on leadership and aggression may become leaders of delinquent peer groups in adoléscence.

In view of the need for affiliation, it is not surprising that a child or teenager who has esteem issues and worries about popularity will take advantage of the internet to forge friendships with those who have a higher social status. At the same time, they can take the opportunity to denigrate and exclude those who they perceive as a threat to their efforts to seek dominance within a group with greater impunity than in face-to-face interactions. If these online interactions take an aggressive form, it is unsurprising that they might be judged as cyberbullying.

Social Skills Training

Social skills training has been found to be effective in helping children and teenagers to increase their popularity. The training can take many forms, from direct coaching to role-playing and showing children films depicting good peer interactions.

A lot of emphasis has been placed on teaching children entry strategies to use when they wish to join a group or enter a cross-membership group. The authors of *The Development of Children's Friendships* are of the opinion that unpopular children behave as if they are newcomers to a group: they tend to hover, waiting longer before making their first move and use more strategies than popular children.[10] An analysis of their entry behaviour showed that they disagreed more, called attention to themselves by stating their feelings and opinions, making self-statements and asking informational questions, which often resulted in them being ignored.

Therefore, unpopular children, summarised by Asher and Gottman as disagreeable, bossy and unable to keep disagreements from escalating, should be encouraged to determine the group's interests, beliefs and values by asking relevant questions of the members. In addition, they need to establish themselves as sharing and agreeing with their interests, rules and sanctions.

When in a disagreement, they should be encouraged to offer up a general rather than a specific reason and provide an alternative course of action.

Clearly, the more socially skilled and emotionally literate children are, the better able they will be to initiate and maintain enduring friendships, and thus fulfil their need for acceptance. Some ways in which parents can help their children become more emotionally literate are:

- Become self-aware: help your child to recognise their own feelings and the feelings of others. Build a vocabulary of words to express feelings and help them choose the appropriate actions to convey the different feelings. Practise making the link between thoughts, feelings and behaviour, as the way we think influences how we feel and in turn determines how we behave
- Manage feelings: encourage your child to develop the art of self-talk. Practise cancelling negative self-messages and substituting them with positive ones (e.g. 'I am calm', 'I am good at ...', 'I am able to ...'). Also help them to recognise the triggers for strong emotions (such as anger, fear and sadness) and to find ways of managing them
- Show social warmth: help your child to express emotions (joy, affection, sympathy) so that they need not hold back if they wish to comfort or support their peers
- Develop self-disclosure: help your child achieve a balance between reluctance to disclose and oversharing, thus risking boring or alienating peers. Self-disclosure reflects desirable traits such as openness, trust, honesty and a lack of defensiveness
- Encourage listening: help your child to listen to peers even if they do not share or are not particularly interested in their views. Being a good listener is as vital to successful social interactions as is having something to say
- Manage stress: Help them recognise the signs and source of stress. Teach them simple relaxation techniques
- Build empathy: take every opportunity to encourage your child to consider others, so they will learn to recognise that everyone thinks and feels differently. This will ease any readiness they may have to pass judgement on peers who hold different views to them. This is especially important now that our schools are becoming more multi-cultural and multi-denominational

- Develop assertiveness: teach your child how to say 'no' and state their case without being unpleasant. They should be comfortable requesting help and expressing positive and negative feelings, as well as starting, carrying out and ending conversations
- Encourage personal responsibility: do not accept excuses for wrongdoing or allow blame to be laid at a sibling or classmate's door
- Encouraging physical activity and sports that have rules and sanctions is also a very good way to help children to mix and network, take responsibility, handle stress, manage emotions, resolve disputes and work co-operatively
- Conflict resolution: encourage and practise a win-win outcome to disagreements and conflicts.[11]

Dealing with the Need for Power

Chapter 4 discussed how the need for power can be a motive for cyberbullying. Power as a motivational need stems from the desire to influence and have an impact on others. People motivated by power are often characterised as enjoying status, recognition, winning arguments and taking risks. There are two kinds of power: social and personal.[12]

A need for social power, commonly referred to as 'socialised power motivation', reflects a desire to make a pro-social impact on others. Thus, decisions that are taken are to serve others' interests. On the other hand, the need for personal power – 'personalised power motivation' – reflects an egotistic desire to make an impact on others with a disregard for their needs and interests. You can probably call to mind many people, past and present, who fit these two types of power motivations. Dictators like Stalin, Hitler and Pol Pot, or cult leaders like Jim Jones, are extreme examples of personalised power motivation. These figures illustrate how power and leadership are not always for the good. Mother Teresa, however, is recognised as having been motivated by social power, showing the positive potential for society when people are driven by a need to help others.

While a distinction was not made between the social and personal when power was identified as a motive for cyberbullying[13] it is unlikely that children with socialised power motivation would engage in cyberbullying. However, individuals with a personal need for power would probably find cyberbullying tactics attractive, as they would allow them to readily score points and get the better of an opponent.[14]

Until such time as more research is forthcoming on the relationship between the need for power and cyberbullying, it would be sensible for parents to reinforce socialised power motivation, encouraging the helping of others. By drawing examples from history or contemporary high-profile cases, parents can demonstrate how putting personal interest ahead of responsibility to society actually means risking popularity and status, only to experience shame and punishment in its place. Using personal power to gain recognition among classmates can backfire, because once deviant behaviour is identified it can lead to shameful behaviour – such as violence – which may impact negatively on the rest of a child's life.

As well as helping children understand the negative consequences of exercising personal power, parents need to provide opportunities so that their children may enjoy recognition and rewards for any pro-social behaviour they exhibit. This means providing plenty of opportunities from which children can draw positive benefits. Too often parents set the bar very high, leaving children feeling that they cannot meet expectations, whether it be in academic or sporting activities. This often leads to feelings of shame, frustration, jealousy and anger, and if a child is the type to externalise their frustrations, this may be expressed as bullying behaviours. The fact that a child participates in and enjoys an activity worthy of recognition in itself, and when they build competence in their chosen activity they will gain in self-efficacy and confidence. To strengthen pro-social behaviour, encourage charity or volunteering work and, where possible, have children help family and friends who may have special needs. The incidental reinforcements that come from such work – for example, the sincere thanks that they so often get and the pride in seeing the positive effect their help has first-hand – will do much to promote their pro-social behaviour.

Chapter 11: Key Messages
- Cyberbullying in childhood and teenage years needs to be nipped in the bud to prevent long-term psychosocial problems for the perpetrators.

- Take a restorative rather than a punitive approach to correcting cyberbullying.
- Support the school's anti-bullying message and promote respect for diversity.
- Look to the underlying motives for cyberbullying. For example, what needs are going unmet in your child?
- Look to ways in which your child can learn to express their frustrations in a more socially acceptable manner.
- Play to your child's strengths and provide opportunities for recognition and achievement.
- Avoid aggressive outbursts and model positive parenting.
- Seek professional help to overcome any emotional and behavioural problems in your child or teenager that may, with your own best efforts, be resistant to change.

Notes

1. From the European *Cyber Training 4 Parents*, with which I was involved: cybertraining4parents.org/ebook/.
2. P. Gradinger, D. Strohmeier and C. Spiel, 'Motives for Bullying Others in Cyberspace: Austria', *Cyberbullying in the Global Playground: Research from International Perspectives*, Q. Li, D. Cross, P. K. Smith, eds (London: Wiley-Blackwell, 2012).
3. American Psychological Association, 'Controlling Anger Before it Controls You', http://apa.org/topics/anger/control.aspx?item=2 (accessed 14 December 2013).
4. Ibid.
5. See *Understanding School Bullying: A Guide for Parents and Teachers*, pp. 217–21, where I deal in some detail with how parents can help children manage their anger.
6. M. O'Moore, 'Cyberbullying: The Situation in Ireland', *Pastoral Care in Education* 30 (2012): pp. 209–23.
7. H. A. Murray, *Explorations in Personality* (New York: Oxford University Press, 1938).
8. J. Harris, cited in P. K. Smith, H. Cowie and M. Blades, *Understanding Children's Development* (London: Blackwell Publishing, 2005).
9. Smith, Cowie and Blades (2005), op. cit.
10. S. R. Asher and J. M. Gottman, *The Development of Children's Friendships* (Cambridge: Cambridge University Press, 1981).
11. Extracted from Smith, Cowie and Blades (2005), op. cit.; and Fontana, *Psychology for Teachers* (London: Palgrave and the British Psychological Society, 1995).
12. D. C. McClelland, 'The Two Faces of Power', *Journal of International Affairs* 24 (1970): pp. 29–47.
13. Gradinger, Strohmeier and Spiel (2012), op. cit.
14. E. M. Fodor and D. P. Wick, 'Need for Power and Affective Response to Negative Audience Reaction to an Extemporaneous Speech', *Journal of Research in Personality* 43.3 (2009): pp. 721–5.

CONCLUSION

While our scientific knowledge of cyberbullying is only emerging, there is strong evidence to suggest that cyberbullying is prevalent among our school-going population, currently peaking in our fifteen- and sixteen-year-olds but with younger and younger children becoming involved. However, by tackling cyberbullying there will be scores of children and teenagers who will be spared the social isolation, emotional distress, depression, poor academic and sporting achievements and self-harming behaviour so commonly associated with cyber-victimisation. Tackling cyberbullying will also save lives; while cyber-victimisation is not always the sole contributory factor in cyberbullying-related suicides, it can be the straw that breaks the camel's back. To be exposed to both cyber and traditional bullying, which is not uncommon, can have a significantly stronger negative impact than being subjected to either form of bullying. Cyberbullying can take the joy out of living and, as Ban Ki-moon stated regarding homophobic bullying, can 'cut promising lives short'. Through tackling cyberbullying, golden opportunities will also arise to identify and correct behaviours that would otherwise place perpetrators at risk of significant negative outcomes as they advance through school and adulthood.[1] Bully-victims, being the most troubled, need early detection. Research, for example, has shown that cyberbullying is not limited to childhood and adolescence but is also evident among third-level students[2] and in the workplace.[3]

The purpose of this book has been to deepen the understanding of cyberbullying and share the key competencies that intervention studies have shown to be effective in preventing and reducing the level of cyberbullying among children and teenagers. With increased awareness and knowledge about cyberbullying and its coping strategies, it is hoped that you, as readers, will take active steps towards countering and preventing it. While the book is predominantly directed at teachers and parents, cyberbullying, like traditional bullying, requires that we all take ownership of the problem and seize every opportunity to discourage it and to support those who are victims of it. Commonly held societal attitudes about cyberbullying – for example, that it is acceptable and part of our online world – must be changed. This requires more people in society, and especially those in authority, to take responsibility and show their disapproval of cyberbullying. If we as adults, and especially teachers, are seen to accept or turn a blind eye to cyberbullying, as highlighted in the book, we cannot expect to influence the behaviour of our young people. In order for normative behaviour to change, we need to amend perceptions, or indeed misperceptions, of behaviour.

Though the book did not deal with the role of the media, internet service providers and popular websites in tackling cyberbullying, it must be stressed that they also have a definite role in the prevention of cyberbullying. The book outlined the potential power of schools to develop social-norm campaigns to increase positive bystander behaviour. The media, internet service providers and popular websites could, for example, invite and/or assist schools in the launch of such campaigns. Young people who are strongly influenced by their peers need to be faced with powerful messages which illustrate that most youths do not cyberbully. It is also vital that these messages are seen to be endorsed by role models to teenagers.

This book promotes a restorative approach to acts of cyberbullying by children and teenagers, arguing that it provides valuable lessons for the cyberbullies. They are made to think through what they have done and to consider the consequences of their behaviour. It also provides them with the opportunity to develop greater tolerance and respect for individual differences. In addition, it helps to develop social skills, in particular feelings of empathy, which are characteristically low in children who bully. Most importantly, restorative approaches to wrongdoing teach the perpetrators to take responsibility for their unacceptable behaviour. Having to offer up suggestions as to how they will refrain from further hurting the victim provides opportunities for them to learn new social strategies that will help them in future to deal with their peers whom they may for whatever reason dislike.

Restorative approaches offer a way to halt the cycle of violence, especially when cyber and traditional bullying is an escalation of tit-for-tat behaviour. Such methods can also provide new ways for parents and teachers to point out and manage the motives for engaging in cyberbullying, such as frustration and anger.

If, in the coming years, campaigns, raising awareness, curricular activities and greater parental knowledge of cyberbullying and our current laws prove to be insufficient in curbing cyberbullying, consideration needs to be given to supporting the introduction of specific laws to criminalise it.

In Part One of the book, I discussed what distinguishes cyberbullying from traditional bullying, the many forms and methods of cyberbullying, the characteristics of those involved and the ill-effects of their involvement as victims, bullies and bully-victims. I also showed that many children do not have the skills to handle cyberbullying and its impact on their lives. Many do not seek help for fear of negative reactions from their peers, as well as from their parents or guardians. There are also many who do not seek help because they have little faith in adults' ability to intervene effectively. Some take a passive stance, ignoring the cyber-attacks or going offline, while others confront the problem in an aggressive manner, leaving themselves open to an escalation of cyberbullying. Moreover, feelings of shame, guilt and embarrassment contribute to children not seeking the necessary support from either their peers or adults, leaving them at risk of social and emotional difficulties, disliking school and displaying self-destructive behaviour.

In Part Two, I argued that schools need to take ownership of cyberbullying to affect change. They are ideally placed to educate all their members, their staff, parents, pupils and the wider community about cyberbullying and to take corrective action when incidents come to their attention.

The book promotes the whole school community approach, which has been endorsed by the new *Anti-Bullying Procedures* launched by the Department of Education and Skills[4] as the most effective way to reach all members of a school community. Guided by the scientific literature and my experience of working with schools, I outlined in some detail four pillars of action that schools need to embrace when implementing the whole school community approach in order to achieve success in reducing their level of cyberbullying.

The first pillar of action is to build and review annually, with the help of the school community members, a cyberbullying policy that is integrated into their formal whole school anti-bullying policy and that outlines the responsibilities of staff, parents and pupils and the wider community with regards to preventing and countering cyberbullying.

The second pillar of action is to raise awareness and educate the whole school community about cyberbullying. This includes providing the teaching and non-teaching staff and the pupils with a thorough understanding of cyberbullying and the key competencies and skills for preventing and dealing with it. To close the generation gap, which so commonly exists between 'digitally native' pupils and their parents, awareness-raising programmes/workshops also need to be made available to parents and guardians.

The third pillar of action is to build collaborative school–family community relations. This involves recognising that teachers, parents and pupils need to work together to make prevention and intervention of cyberbullying a shared responsibility. Schools need to encourage the reporting of cyberbullying by its members, as well as regularly seeking their opinions when their cyberbullying policy and practices are under review. Also, often due to limited resources, schools need to form partnerships with professionals in the areas of both mental health and information and communication to meet ongoing needs for counselling or social skills training, or the removal of offensive content from websites.

The fourth pillar of action is for schools to build a positive and supportive school climate that promotes diversity and respect for individual differences, as well as a sense of belonging and connectedness with the school. In order for children and teenagers to open up to one another, and indeed to staff, about sensitive issues such as cyberbullying, they need to feel safe. Relationship building between staff, pupils and parents is critical to achieve the desired supportive social environment. Teachers must maintain warm positive relations with all pupils. This can more easily be achieved by promoting restorative approaches to wrongdoing rather than committing to harsh discipline policies. Also, providing a range of extra-curricular activities that allow children to develop and demonstrate competence and build relationships with their peers and staff outside of the classroom will enhance school connectedness and protect children from engaging in health-risk behaviours such as cyberbullying.

The importance of school connectedness is illustrated by Tim Hands, the principal of Magdalen College School in Oxford. When recently asked how he attributed the fact that his school achieved the top ranking for the southeast of England he replied that the achievement came as no surprise to him. He attributed the school's success to the attention it pays to making sure that the children are happy above all. His words were, 'it's old fashioned but our interest is in children being happy first and foremost, and academic, sporting, musical and artistic success follows from that. Paying attention to children's pastoral care is an old and enduring value and it is our primary focus'.[5]

In addition to addressing the role of schools in the prevention and intervention of cyberbullying, the book has identified several practical steps that teachers and parents need to take in order to a) motivate children and teenagers to refrain from engaging in cyberbullying and b) give them the knowledge so that they may cope effectively should they ever be victimised or be witness to a cyberbullying incident.

Part Two of the book also emphasises what teachers can do. They hold the key to engaging their pupils in curricular activities that will provide them with good internet safety skills, good social skills, inclusive of good ethical behaviour when online (netiquette), and critically providing them with effective coping strategies in the face of cyber-victimisation.

Part Three of the book also concentrates on the role of the family in prevention and intervention of cyberbullying. It discusses the important role that parents have in finding the balance between being the 'snooper' or 'helicopter' parent and that of taking a trusting stance on their children and teenagers' online behaviour. While age will determine what level of supervision and monitoring of internet use is necessary, I have stressed the need for and the ways in which parents can keep abreast of the rapidly evolving digital technology that their children will use for good and for bad.

Attention is also given in Part Three to the role that parents can play in helping children become more open about their own problems of cyber-victimisation and also about how they can look out for and become an active defender of peers who are subjected to cyber-attacks. In recognising that prevention is better than cure and in acknowledging that more research is needed for definitive recommendations to be made, the book shares information as to how parents can best help their children to escape unscathed from potential cyber-attacks. How cyberbullying impacts on a child or teenager will depend on the type of bullying, the duration, the intensity, their psychological sturdiness, their attachment to parent and family, their connectedness to the school and their level of social support. Among the important attributes to be nurtured by parents are resilience, self-esteem and good social skills. Based on our most recent research the dominant motives for cyberbullying – anger, fun, affiliation and power – are discussed, along with the valuable role that parents can play in helping their children avoid becoming involved in cyberbullying, whether as bullies or bully-victims.

Also pertinent to preventing and dealing with cyberbullying is an understanding of the legal implications it has. The book, therefore, has devoted a special chapter to this topic, written by Murray Smith, a barrister of Irish Law. It is found in the Appendix of the book.

Finally, in recognising the attraction and enormous social and educational value of the internet for children and adults alike, I hope that this book will go some way to give you, as a reader, the knowledge, determination and confidence to tackle and prevent cyberbullying, whether it occurs in or outside of our schools. Your action alone can make all the difference to the health and safety of our school-going children and teenagers in the years ahead.

Notes

1. M. M. Ttofi, D. P. Farrington and F. Losel, 'Interrupting the Continuity from School Bullying to Later Internalising and Externalising Problems: Findings from Cross-National Comparative Studies', *Journal of School Violence*, 13 (2014): pp. 1–4.
2. L. McGuire, 'Third-Level Students' Experiences of Bullying in Ireland', *Bullying in Irish Education: Perspectives in Research and Practice*, M. O'Moore and P. Stevens, eds (Cork: Cork University Press, 2013): pp. 100–23.
3. P. Stevens, 'The Bullying of Primary School Principals in Ireland', *Bullying in Irish Education: Perspectives in Research and Practice*, M. O'Moore, and P. Stevens, eds (Cork: Cork University Press, 2013): pp. 177–209.
4. Department of Education and Skills, *Anti-Bullying Procedures for Primary and Post-Primary Schools*, http://www.education.ie/en/Publications/Policy-Reports/Anti-Bullying-Procedures-for-Primary-and-Post-Primary-Schools.pdf (2013).
5. Sian Griffiths, 'Old-school principles come out on top', *Sunday Times* (13 July 2014).

APPENDIX

Cyberbullying and the Law

SOME LAW ON CYBERBULLYING

Murray Smith

This chapter looks at some law on cyberbullying, including an official definition; the possible legal consequences of cyberbullying by people under eighteen; the legal responsibilities of their parents or guardians for that behaviour; and the legal responsibilities of schools for it, including if it happens outside of school hours.

The Oireachtas Joint Committee of Transport and Communications, in their July 2013 report, *Addressing the Growth of Social Media and Tackling Cyberbullying*, looked at existing legislation. While it found that the legislation encompassed some online offences, it discovered that there were difficulties in legislating for some online behaviour.[1]

For reasons of space I will discuss only parts of the legal framework in this country. If you wish for greater detail, please refer to my chapter in *Bullying in Irish Education*.[2] It should be noted also that an overview of the law in any area, and in any country, can quickly become out of date, and for that reason what I write here is not a substitute for getting present-day legal advice on this subject. In addition, while the law may deter cyberbullying from taking place, and when it happens, provide a framework for punishment or financial compensation, it is not a complete solution to it.

What is 'Cyberbullying'?

There is no legal definition of 'cyberbullying', but there is an official one in *A Guide to Cyberbullying*, part of the *Get With It!* series of publications, joint initiatives of the Office of Internet Safety, an executive office of the Department of Justice, Barnardos, O$_2$, and the National Centre for Technology in Education. Essentially it finds support in the research literature as discussed in Chapter 1, namely that:

> Cyberbullying refers to bullying which is carried out using the internet, mobile phone or other technological devices. Cyberbullying

generally takes a psychological rather than physical form but is often part of a wider pattern of 'traditional' bullying. It can take the form of sending nasty, mean or threatening messages, emails, photos or video clips; silent phone calls; putting up nasty posts or pictures on a message board, website or chat room; saying hurtful things in a chat room; pretending to be someone else in a chat room or message board or text message and saying hurtful things; or accessing someone's accounts to make trouble for them.[3]

Some Criminal and Civil Law

The law in Ireland can be generally divided up into two parts: *criminal law*, the law about actions (or failures to act) forbidden by the State, with punishment as a sanction; and *civil law*, the law about resolving disputes between private individuals and organisations, providing a remedy, usually financial, against the wrongdoer as compensation, not punishment.[4] In criminal law, the State makes a decision to bring or not to bring a prosecution against a person or organisation; and in civil law, a private person or organisation makes a decision to bring a case against at least one other private person or organisation.

a. Three criminal law statutes

Much of the criminal law is set out in statutory form, a statute being a law passed by both houses of the Oireachtas and signed into law by the president. Three statutes are relevant here.

i. Post Office Amendment Act 1951

Section 13(1) of this Act says that any person commits a criminal offence who sends by telephone 'any message that is grossly offensive, or is indecent, obscene or menacing' or 'for the purpose of causing annoyance, inconvenience, or needless anxiety' to another person, that person either sends by telephone any message 'that the sender knows to be false', or 'persistently makes telephone calls to another person without reasonable cause'.

Due to the advent of the smartphone version of the mobile telephone, a 'message' could include any communication sent by a person or group to another person or group from such a telephone.

On *summary conviction*, a criminal conviction after a hearing before a judge only, or a *conviction on indictment*, a criminal conviction after a hearing before both a judge and jury, that person can be imprisoned for up to twelve months or up to five years respectively, fined or both.

ii. Criminal Damage Act 1991

There are two relevant parts here: a) threat to damage property; and b) unauthorised accessing of data. The first part (Section 3) says that a person commits a criminal offence if, without lawful excuse, he or she 'makes to another a threat, intending that that other [person] would fear it would be carried out', either to damage 'any property belonging to that other person or a third person', or to damage his or her own property 'in a way which he knows is likely to endanger the life of that other or a third person'.

On summary conviction, such a person can be fined, imprisoned for up to twelve months, or both, and on conviction on indictment can be fined, imprisoned for up to ten years, or both.

The second part (Section 5) says that a person who 'without lawful use' operates a computer inside the State 'with intent to access any data kept either within or outside the State', or outside the State 'with intent to access any data kept within the State', shall, 'whether or not he accesses any data', be guilty of a criminal offence.

On summary conviction, that person can be fined, imprisoned for up to three months, or both. This was intended to deal with computer hacking, but is obviously relevant here.

iii. Non-Fatal Offences Against the Person Act 1997

There are two offences under this Act that overlap with cyberbullying: a) threats to kill or cause serious harm; and b) harassment. About the first, Section 5 says that a person who, without lawful excuse, 'makes to another a threat, by any means intending the other to believe it will be carried out, to kill or cause serious harm to that other or a third person shall be guilty of an offence'. A person guilty of this offence shall be liable on summary conviction to a fine, imprisonment for up to twelve months, or both; and on conviction on indictment, to a fine, imprisonment for a term of up to ten years, or both.

The second offence, harassment, under Section 10, says that any person who, without lawful authority or reasonable excuse, 'by any means *including by use of the telephone*, harasses another by persistently following, watching, pestering, besetting or communicating with him or her', shall be guilty of a criminal offence.[5]

A person harasses another by his or her acts, intentional or reckless, when he or she 'seriously interferes with the other's peace and privacy or causes alarm, distress or harm to the other', and these acts are 'such that a reasonable person would realise that the acts would seriously interfere with the other's peace and privacy or cause alarm, distress or harm to the other'.

As well as imprisonment, a fine or both, whether on summary conviction (up to twelve months) or conviction on indictment (up to seven years), a court may also, or as an alternative, order that the person shall not, for a specified period, 'communicate by any means with the other person or that the person shall not approach within such distance as the court shall specify of the place of residence or employment of the other person'.

b. Civil law

In civil law, there is an area called *tort*, a tort being a wrong that is a breach of a duty imposed by the law on a person or organisation, the main remedy for a breach of such duty being damages. In tort, the purpose is to restore the injured party to the position he or she was in, as if no wrong took place. The main torts include negligence and defamation.

i. Negligence

Negligence is a breach of a legal duty of care where damage is caused to the party to whom that duty is owed. It has four main elements:

a. A duty of care between the parties, of a particular standard
b. A failure to observe this
c. Actual loss or damage, including personal injury
d. A 'sufficiently close causal connection' between the failure and the injury.

The law recognises that many persons and organisations owe a duty of care to others. The standard of care expected is that of an 'ordinary or prudent man'.[6]

This standard of care, imposed by the courts on a person or organisation, depends on those towards whom it owes a duty. For example, an employer has a greater standard of care towards employees depending on their ages, their levels of experience, and the nature of their jobs. The standard of care imposed by the courts on schools towards their students is that of a 'prudent parent'; or it is sometimes said that schools are *in loco parentis* (in the place of a parent) when children are in their care. This prudent parent standard of care was first developed in an English case, *Williams v. Eady*,[7] a judgment that has been followed by the Irish courts.

The body responsible for a school's duty of care is stated by Section 15 of the Education Act 1998 to be its board of management, which is to manage the school 'for the benefit of the students and their parents'. Section 23 of the Education (Welfare) Act 2000 states that a school has to draw up a 'code of behaviour' regarding its students. In guidelines issued by the National Educational Welfare Board in 2008 on how to draw up such a code, the NEWB said that a school's board of management 'must have policies to prevent bullying and harassment'.[8]

The *Anti-Bullying Procedures for Primary and Post-Primary Schools*, referred to earlier in this book, give direction and guidance to school authorities in dealing with bullying, which explicitly includes cyberbullying. They explicitly state that all schools are required to have an anti-bullying policy within their codes of behaviour.[9]

A case for personal injury resulting from negligence can only be taken within two years of the date of injury or date of knowledge of the injury, whichever is the later.[10] In most cases, the date of injury and date of knowledge will be the same. In the case of someone under eighteen, the legal date of knowledge is his or her eighteenth birthday. However, before he or she turns that age, a case can be taken on that person's behalf by a parent or guardian.

ii. Defamation Act 2009

The tort of defamation is regulated by a statute, the Defamation Act 2009. Section 6(2) of that Act defines 'defamation' as publication of a 'defamatory statement' about a person to at least one other person. A 'defamatory statement' is defined as 'a statement that tends to injure a person's reputation in the eyes of reasonable members of society, and "defamatory" shall be construed accordingly'. A 'defamation action' is defined as '(a) an action for damages for defamation, or (b) an application for a declaratory order, whether or not a claim for other relief under this Act is made'.

In terms of remedies, a person who claims to be the subject of a statement alleged to be defamatory may apply to the Circuit Court for an order that the statement is 'false and defamatory of him or her'. The High Court, or the relevant court where the defamation case has been brought, can make an order 'prohibiting the publication or further publication' of the relevant statement if, in its opinion, the statement was defamatory, and the defendant has no defence that is 'reasonably likely to succeed'.

A defamation action cannot be brought later than a year 'from the date on which the cause of action accrued', unless the court grants leave for a period of up to two years.

Defences under the Act include:

a. 'Truth' (Where 'the statement in respect of which the action was brought is true in all material respects')
b. Privilege, both 'absolute' and 'qualified'
c. 'Honest opinion' (Where 'in the case of a statement consisting of an opinion, the opinion was honestly held')
d. 'Apology' (Not a defence strictly speaking, but can be used as a defence in mitigation [reduction] of damages)
e. 'Consent' (Where it can be proved that the plaintiff consented to the publication of the relevant statement)
f. 'Fair and reasonable publication on a matter of public interest'
g. 'Innocent publication' (Where the person says he or she was not the author, editor or publisher of the statement, he or she took reasonable care in its publication, and did not know or believe that he or she contributed to the publication of a statement that could give rise to a defamation case).

This matter is relevant to the question of cyberbullying, because it is quite possible that an aggrieved student, or someone on his or her behalf, may not just sue another student and a parent or guardian, but also the relevant internet service provider or those responsible for websites, including social-networking ones, arguing that they are the publisher of the relevant defamatory statement or statements posted on it.

iii. Remedies

The main remedy, for someone taking a negligence or defamation case, is *damages*, already mentioned. There is, however, a problem if the student accused of cyberbullying that comes under these torts, or that person's parent or guardian, does not have the ability to pay any damages awarded. This is why a school, an internet service provider, or someone responsible for a website, tend to be sued for damages on their own, or in addition to the student, or his or her parent or guardian; they can better afford to pay the damages.

Instead of damages, a person taking a case can look instead for an *injunction*, an order of the court to a particular individual or organisation to do something or not to do something. An injunction can be granted by a court if it is satisfied that damages would not be an adequate remedy. For example, it may be an adequate remedy if abusive material is posted online about a person, and that person, or someone on his or her behalf, wants an injunction that the relevant person or organisation remove that material, something financial compensation cannot do.

c. Data Protection Acts 1988 and 2003

These Acts uphold the right to privacy for people in relation to their 'personal data'. This is data about a living individual who 'is or can be identified', either from the data (on computer or on paper files) or 'in conjunction with other information that is in, or is likely to come into, the possession of the data controller'. A 'data controller' is a person who, alone or with others 'controls the contents or use of personal data', while a 'data processor' is a person who processes personal data on behalf of a data controller, not including an employee of the latter.

171

A data controller, under Section 2, has an obligation to ensure that such data has been:

a. Fairly obtained and fairly processed
b. Accurate and complete, and where necessary kept up to date
c. Obtained for one or more explicit and legitimate purposes
d. Not processed in a manner incompatible with that purpose or purposes
e. Is adequate, relevant and not excessive regarding those purposes, and not kept longer than necessary for those purposes.

A person has the right to establish if another person keeps personal data by writing to them to be so informed, and to be also given a description of the data and the purpose for which it is kept, being told this within twenty-one days of the request being given or sent.

A person has the right of access to such data, with certain exceptions. He or she has the right to write to the data controller for such data to be rectified, blocked or erased, if it contravenes Section 2, the data controller needing to comply no more than forty days after it has been given or sent. He or she also has the right to request the latter to cease processing such data if it causes 'substantial damage or distress to him or her or another person', and such damage or distress would be 'unwarranted'.

It is made clear for the law of torts that a person being a data controller or data processor shall 'owe a duty of care to the data subject concerned'.

There is an independent official called the Data Protection Commissioner, who has the power to investigate any contraventions of the Acts. When a complaint has been made, the commissioner shall investigate it, unless it is frivolous or vexatious. If unable to arrange an 'amicable resolution' between the parties, the commissioner will notify the complainant in writing of his or her decision, about which the complainant can appeal to the Circuit Court within twenty-one days. The commissioner can serve an 'enforcement notice' on a data controller found to have violated Section 2 to 'block, rectify, erase or destroy' any of the relevant data. The person concerned may appeal this order to the Circuit Court within twenty-one days. On compliance of the data controller, he or she shall notify the complaintant of the data's blocking, rectification, erasure or destruction within forty days.

The Data Protection Acts and the *Electronic Communications Regulations* (S.I. 336 of 2011) set out the rules that data controllers must obey. Breaches of these rules sometimes involve offences that are punishable by fines. Summary proceedings can be brought by the commissioner, the punishment being a fine of €5,000. On indictment, the fines range from up to €50,000 if a person, to up to €250,000 if a corporate body.

A person can therefore write to know if personal data is being held on him or her. If he or she feels that a data controller has details about him or her that are not factually correct, the latter can be asked to change or remove such details. He or she can also request that processing of personal data cease if it is likely to cause 'substantial damage or distress'. If this does not happen, the person can complain to the Data Protection Commissioner. A case under the tort of negligence can also be taken against the data controller.

As can be seen, use of these Acts can be made by someone against an internet service provider or someone responsible for a website, if any of the latter have, as a result of cyberbullying, control of the former's personal data.

Responsibility of Young People Under the Criminal Law

Here, I will look at how the criminal law treats those under eighteen. While twelve is the age of criminal responsibility, those between twelve and eighteen years of age are not immune to the effects of the criminal law; and their parents or guardians may, as I will later show, also face legal sanctions due to the criminal offences of their children. Even if criminal charges are not brought, the threat of this happening may be enough in some situations, including school-bullying related ones. Also, there are provisions for dealing with 'anti-social behaviour' by those in that age group, without recourse to the criminal law.

i. General provisions

In terms of when a 'child', defined by the law as a person under eighteen years of age, is responsible for a criminal offence, Section 52

173

of the Children Act 2001, amended by Section 129 of the Criminal Justice Act 2006, states that a child under twelve 'shall not be charged with an offence', the exceptions being a child of eleven to twelve charged with murder, manslaughter, rape and aggravated sexual assault. Also, if any child under fourteen is charged with an offence, 'no further proceedings in the matter', with two exceptions, shall be taken except by or with the consent of the Director of Public Prosecutions.

Children under twelve do not, however, enjoy total immunity from action being taken against them. Section 53 of the 2001 Act, amended by Section 130 of the 2006 Act, says that where a member of the Garda Síochána has 'reasonable grounds' for believing that a child under twelve has committed an offence (apart from the exceptions) that member shall 'endeavour to take the child to the child's parent or guardian' or arrange for another member to do so.

Where this is not possible, such as that member having 'reasonable grounds for believing that the child is not receiving adequate care or protection', the member shall inform the health board for the area in which the child normally resides of the name, address and age of the child and the circumstances in which he or she came to the notice of the Garda Síochána.

Where 'not practicable' for the child to be taken to his or her parent or guardian, the member concerned may give the child, or arrange for the child to be given, into the custody of the health board for the area in which the child normally resides.

The Children Court (the District Court when dealing with children) has the power to impose a number of orders, under the heading of a 'community sanction', on a child found guilty of an offence. They include a day care centre order, probation orders and a restriction of movement order.

The Act allows a court to impose on a child a 'children detention order', that is, 'a period of detention in a children detention school or children detention centre specified in the order'. However, a court will not impose such an order 'unless it is satisfied that detention is the only suitable way of dealing with the child' and, if the child is under sixteen, 'that a place in a children detention school is available for him or her'.

ii. Anti-Social Behaviour

Part 13 of the Criminal Justice Act 2006 introduced new provisions into the criminal law for dealing with children between twelve and eighteen years of age. They allow the Garda Síochána to deal with 'anti-social behaviour'. This is behaviour that happens if a child 'causes, or is likely to cause', to one or more people, not in the same household: (a) harassment, (b) significant or persistent alarm, fear or intimidation, or (c) significant or persistent enjoyment of their property.

Dealing with anti-social behaviour includes:

- Issuing 'behaviour warnings' to children: This is a statement by a member of the Garda Síochána that a child behaved in an anti-social manner, giving details, and demanding that he or she cease such behaviour. It notices that a failure to comply or other anti-social behaviour may result in an application for a behaviour order (Section 160)
- Convening meetings to discuss a child's anti-social behaviour: This can be done by a Garda superintendent, if satisfied a child behaved in an anti-social manner, whether a behaviour warning was issued or not. The child, his or her parents or guardian and others shall be asked to attend. At the meeting, if the child and parents or guardian give undertaking to prevent a recurrence of such behaviour, they shall be asked to enter into a 'good behaviour contract', including these undertakings (Section 161)
- Applying to the courts for a 'behaviour order' in respect of a child: This is if the child continues to behave in an anti-social manner and likely to do so. This order can prohibit the child behaving in a specified manner, and if appropriate, at or in the vicinity of a specified place. The child also has to comply with the specified requirements, and the supervision of the child has to be provided for (Section 162).

All of these provisions are designed to allow the Gardaí to deal effectively with anti-social behaviour while keeping the child out of the criminal justice system.

Responsibilities of Responsible Adults

The answer to whether the parents and guardians of those under eighteen are immune from the criminal offences or torts of their children is 'no'. In certain circumstances, the courts can impose penalties on parents or guardians under the criminal law, and they may be successfully sued in negligence for allowing their child to injure another.

a. Criminal law

The Children Court has the power to impose a number of orders on the parents or guardians of a child found guilty of a criminal offence. These include a 'parental supervision order' of up to six months, ordering them to undergo treatment, participate in a parenting skills course, 'adequately and properly' control or supervise the child and comply with any other instructions to prevent the child committing further offences. Failure to observe such an order may be treated as contempt of court, for which a fine or a jail sentence may be imposed.

The court can also order the payment of compensation by those it feels 'a wilful failure' to care for or control the child contributed to his or her criminal behaviour; or order instead or as well that a parent or guardian enter a recognisance (a promise to the court) to 'exercise proper and adequate control over the child'. Refusal to make this promise may be seen as a contempt of court.

b. Civil law: Tort

The parents or guardians of students who cyberbully can be liable in negligence, as well as schools. A textbook on the law of torts points out that while there is 'no general rule' for parents being liable for the torts of their children, they may be negligent in allowing a child the 'opportunity to injure another'.[11] Three types of behaviour may result in this liability:

i. Dangerous Things

It may be negligent for a person to have dangerous things within reach of a child where it is foreseeable that they would cause injury to that child or another. *Williams v. Eady* showed this, when phosphorous was left within reach of a child by a schoolmaster exercising parental responsibility. An Irish case showed this regarding a gun: *Sullivan v. Creed*.[12] The defendant left his gun loaded and at full cock, ready to fire. His fifteen-year-old son, unaware of this, pointed it at the plaintiff in play and accidentally shot him. The plaintiff successfully sued the father for the injuries caused by the son.[13]

ii. Dangerous Propensities

A parent may be liable if he or she knows or ought to know of a 'dangerous propensity' of a child, and fails to reasonably protect others against an injury resulting from it. Examples include a child previously attacking other people, stealing or damaging property. The steps parents will be required to take will depend on the facts of the case, including the age of the child and the nature of the danger. They will not be liable if their reasonable best was not enough to prevent an injury.[14]

iii. Failure to Control a Child Properly

When parents fail to control a child properly, they may be liable for the child's injuries, or the injuries caused to others. This was particularly stated in the Supreme Court case of *Curley v. Mannion*, where a twelve-year-old girl opened the door of a parked car, driven by her father, in the path of a passing cyclist. In the court's judgment, Chief Justice Ó Dálaigh said 'a parent, while not liable for the torts of his child, may be liable if negligent in failing to exercise his control to prevent his child injuring others'.[15]

All this means is that parents and guardians can be liable in negligence of their minor children if they cyberbully, in the same way schools have, who were acting with delegated parental authority. This can also extend to any tort of defamation carried out by their children, including cyberbullying. For example, did a child commit cyberbullying using the electronic device of a parent or guardian? Even if he or she did so with his or her own electronic device, did the parent or guardian in both cases exercise adequate supervision in how the device was used?

Schools: Duty of Care and What Happens Outside School

As mentioned before, schools have, by law, a duty of care towards their students, comparable to that of a 'prudent parent'. This includes dealing with bullying, including cyberbullying on school grounds, during school hours and using school property. It also includes when outside the school grounds and school hours, such as on a school trip or when a student is representing the school.

I will present four scenarios, then look at the school's legal obligations in each.

Scenario 1

This concerns a student involved in behaviour contrary to the school's rules and code of behaviour *at any time and place*, even when he or she is not identifiable as a student, or is not representing the school. One example is a case of two secondary students expelled from their school for taking drugs at a private party, due to infringing the school rules, which prohibited them taking 'an illicit drug at any time'. Of interest was that it was the severity of the school's punishment that was the issue in the case, not the school's right to punish.[16]

Scenario 2

It concerns a student involved in behaviour that is, first, a breach of the school's rules and code of behaviour; or second, would bring the school's reputation into disrepute. The student is identifiable as a student of the specific school, or is representing the school. This behaviour can include behaviour towards a third party, a fellow student or a school staff member, and may include bullying.[17]

Scenario 3

This happens when there is bad behaviour by one student against another, contrary to the school's rules and code of behaviour at any time and place, regardless of whether the badly behaved student is identifiable as such. A school may be obliged to intervene if the behaviour outside of the school carries on inside the school.[18]

Scenario 4

This involves behaviour by students in the immediate vicinity of a school, both in time and place. While there is no explicit case obliging a school to intervene, there are three cases that have upheld the right of a school to discipline students for such behaviour, and supported the right of a parent to take a case for negligence against a school where a student was physically injured outside of the school, alleging a lack of supervision or an inadequate safety system.[19]

Scenario 1 is completely discretionary in terms of the school's duty of care. A school *may* intervene if it wants, but it is under no legal obligation to do so. Regarding Scenarios 2–4, a school *may be obliged*, under its duty of care, to intervene, if the bullying outside carried over into the school, and if it took place in the immediate vicinity of the school.

In order to deal with any confusion, a school should, in its code of behaviour or anti-bullying policy, make it clear when it will intervene, in terms of disciplining behaviour by students outside the school, outside of school hours, and that it be consistent in enforcing such discipline.

Conclusion

While the law I mentioned may deter cyberbullying, or may provide a framework for punishment or financial compensation if it happens, it is not a complete solution. It is certainly no substitute for those under eighteen, and those with responsibility for them, including parents and guardians, being sufficiently educated to begin to deal with cyberbullying situations. As I mentioned, schools have their specific obligations to deal with cyberbullying, which they may extend if they wish.

If a person, on his or her own behalf, or on behalf of someone else, wants to take a civil case of tort or negligence, it should be seen as a last resort. There is nothing stopping anyone from looking for legal advice, on cyberbullying or any other situation, the person making sure he or she has gathered as much information as possible.

In giving advice, a lawyer will be expected to discourage a person from taking a case, unless all earlier options have been exhausted. Abraham Lincoln, a successful lawyer who became sixteenth President of the United States of America, gave this professional and moral advice for someone intent on a legal career:

Discourage litigation. Persuade your neighbours to compromise whenever you can. Point out to them how the nominal winner is often a real loser – in fees, expenses and waste of time. As a peacemaker the lawyer has a superior opportunity of being a good man. There will be business enough.[20]

Apart from this, a lawyer will point out to someone looking for advice that a person taking a case will need to show that he or she had been reasonable in trying to resolve matters, and the opponent unreasonable. A court will ask for evidence that earlier steps have been taken, such as requests to a school to properly investigate allegations of cyberbullying under its code of behaviour, requests to an internet service provider or person controlling a website to properly deal with abusive material posted online, or both.

Again, I point out that while it is important for all to understand the law around cyberbullying, it is equally important to understand that taking a civil case should, in this area as in others, be a last resort, and that every other means short of this be taken.

Notes

1. Oireachtas Joint Committee of Transport and Communications, *Addressing the Growth of Social Media and Tackling Cyberbullying* (July 2013), www.oireachtas.ie/ parliament/media/Report-on-Social-Media-July-2013-Website.pdf.
2. M. Smith, 'School Bullying and Some Law', *Bullying in Irish Education*, M. O'Moore and P. Stevens, eds (Cork: Cork University Press, 2013), pp. 402–95.
3. *A Guide to Cyberbullying* (Dublin: Brunswick Press, 2008), p. 3. A copy can be downloaded from the website of the Office for Internet Safety at www. internetsafety.ie/website/ois/oisweb.nsf/page/DPCY-7LYJ4V1343473-en/$File/ Finalpercent20-per cent20Lowper cent20Res.pdf.
4. *Murdoch's Dictionary of Irish Law*, fifth edition (Haywards Heath: Tottel Publishing, 2009), p. 302, 190.
5. My italics.
6. *Murdoch's Dictionary of Irish Law*, pp. 1213, 818–9; B. M. E. McMahon and W. Binchy, *Law of Torts*, fourth edition (Haywards Heath: Bloomsbury Professional, 2013), p. 7.
7. *Williams v. Eady*, 10 TLR (1893–94), 41.
8. National Educational Welfare Board, *Drafting a Code of Behaviour: Guidelines for Schools* (2008), www.newb.ie/downloads/pdf/guidelines_school_codes_eng.pdf.
9. Department of Education and Skills, *Anti-Bullying Procedures for Primary and Post-Primary Schools* (2013), www.education.ie/en/Publications/Policy-Reports/ Anti-Bullying-Procedures-for-Primary-and-Post-Primary-Schools.pdf.
10. Civil Liability and Courts Act 2004, Section 7.
11. McMahon and Binchy (2013), op. cit., p. 631.
12. *Sullivan v. Creed* (1904), 2 I.R., 317.

13. McMahon and Binchy (2013), op. cit., pp. 631–2.
14. Ibid., pp. 632–3.
15. *Curley v. Mannion* (1965), I.R., 543 at 546; McMahon and Binchy (2013), op. cit., p. 633.
16. Student A. and Student B. v. Dublin Secondary School (1999), IEHC 47.
17. A Mother and Son v. A Secondary School (DEC-S2004-028).
18. While there are no Irish cases on this scenario, there are a couple of English ones: *R v. London Borough of Newham and Another ex parte X* (1995), ELR, 303; and *Leah Bradford-Smart v. West Sussex County Council* (2002), 1 FCR, 425, which the Irish courts could find persuasive.
19. *The State (Derek Smullen and Declan Smullen) v. Duffy and Others* (1980), I.L.R.M., 46; *Shane Dolan v. Timothy Keohane and Michael Cunningham* (Supreme Court, Unreported, 8 February 1994); *Christina Hosty v. Patrick McDonagh, Canon Hyland and Another* (Supreme Court, Unreported, 29 May 1973).
20. *Collected Works of Abraham Lincoln*, Volume 2 (New Brunswick, NJ: Rutgers University Press, 1953), p. 81.

RESOURCES

Recommended Reading

Amichai-Hamburger, Y., ed., *The Social Net: Understanding Our Online Behaviour*, Second Edition, Oxford: Oxford University Press, 2013

Guidelines for Preventing Cyberbullying in the School Environment: A Review and Recommendations https://sites.google.com/site/costiso801/guideline

Hunter, N., *Internet Safety*, Oxford: Raintree, 2012

Katz, A., *Cyberbullying and E-Safety: What Educators and Other Professionals Need to Know*, London: Jessica Kingsley Publishers, 2012

Kirwan, G. and Power, A., *Cybercrime: The Psychology of Online Offenders*, Cambridge: Cambridge University Press, 2013

Kowalski, R. M., Limber, S. P. and Agatston, P. W., *Cyberbullying: Bullying in the Digital Age*, Second Edition, New Jersey: Wiley-Blackwell, 2012

Li, Q., Cross, D. and Smith, P. K., eds, *Cyberbullying in the Global Playground: Research from International Perspectives*, New Jersey: Wiley-Blackwell, 2012

Mora-Merchan, J. A. and Jäger, T., eds, *Cyberbullying: A Cross-national Comparison*, Landau: Verlag Empirische Pädagogik, 2010

O'Moore, M. and James Minton, S., *Cyber-Bullying: The Irish Experience*, New York: Nova Science Publishers, 2011

O'Moore, M. and Stevens, P., eds, *Bullying in Irish Education: Perspectives in Research and Practice*, Cork: Cork University Press, 2013

Philips, R., Linney, J. and Pack, C., *Safe School Ambassadors: Harnessing Student Power to Stop Bullying and Violence*, San Francisco: Jossey-Bass, 2007

Rogers, V., *Cyberbullying: Activities to Help Children and Teens To Stay Safe in a Texting, Twittering, Social Networking World*, London: Jessica Kingsley Publishers, 2010

Shariff, S., *Confronting Cyber-Bullying: What Schools Need to Know to Control Misconduct and Avoid Legal Consequences*, Second Edition, Cambridge: Cambridge University Press, 2011

Smith, P. K. and Steffgen, G., eds, *Cyberbullying Through the New Media: Findings from an International Network*, Oxford: Psychology Press, 2013

Trolley, B. C. and Hanel, C., *Cyber Kids, Cyber Bullying, Cyber Balance*, CA: Corwin, 2010

Online Resources and Tools for Parents and Teachers
A guide to cyberbullying: www.internetsafety.ie

Get With It!
- A Guide to Cyberbullying
- A Parents' Guide to Social Networking Websites
- A Parents' Guide to Filtering Technologies
- A Parents' Guide to New Media Technologies.

Found at: http://www.internetsafety.ie/website/ois/oisweb.nsf/page/publications-en

Anti-Bullying Ambassadors: You can watch a short YouTube video of their work in Northern Ireland and Republic of Ireland schools at http://youtu.be/Z3-gGhou0F4

Anti-Bullying Campaign – Tools for Teachers: www.antibullyingcampaign.ie

Coping with bullying – support for children, teenagers and parents: www.barnardos.ie

Cybertraining for Parents (CT4P) – A Self-directed Course for Trainers and Parents: cybertraining4parents.org/ebook/

Educational resources for parents and teachers: www.webwise.ie

Managing children's profiles on social-networking sites: www.watchyourspace.ie

Parents' Guide to Mobile Phones: www.hotline.ie/library/knowledge.pdf

Guidelines for Preventing Cyberbullying in the School Environment – A Review and Recommendations: https://sites.google.com/site/costiso801/guideline

Safe to Learn – Embedding Anti-Bullying Work in Schools: www.schools-out.org.uk/policy/docs/DCSF_homophobic_bullying/summary_safe_to_learn.pdf

Vista, Violence in Schools Training Action – A whole school community approach to bullying: www.vista-europe.org

Audio-Visual Resources

ARBAX, a 3D video game on racial bullying and xenophobia, to be used by young people of secondary school age. Also features teacher guidelines: www.schoolbullying.eu/doc/ARBAX. This is multilateral project, funded by a grant from the European Union Lifelong Learning Programme

Let's Fight it Together, a short film: http://old.digizen.org/cyberbullying/fullfilm.aspx. Developed by Childnet International and the Department of Education in the UK

Silent Witnesses, a DVD to stimulate all forms of discussion, especially on how bystanders can become more responsible: www.dcu.ie/abc. Produced by the Anti-Bullying Centre

Speak Out: A DVD Resource to Help Recognise and Deal with School Bullying, a DVD resource for use in talking to students about bullying and the many forms it can take, using acted-out scenarios. Tom Gunning, Siobhan O'Donoghue and Loreto Secondary School, Wexford (Veritas, 2002)

Stand Up, a thirteen-minute DVD on homophobic and transphobic bullying: www.belongto.org. Developed by Belong and Department of Education and Skills

Useful Websites for Advice and Guidance
For Parents
www.dcu.ie/abc
www.barnardos.ie
www.childline.ie
www.watchyourspace.ie
www.webwise.ie

For Schools
www.dcu.ie/abc
www.ncte.ie
www.scoilnet.ie
www.thinkb4uclick.ie
www.watchyourspace.ie
www.webwise.ie

Internet Safety
www.hotline.ie
www.internetsafety.ie
www.webwise.ie

For Children and Teenagers
www.spunout.ie
www.tacklebullying.ie
www.watchyourspace.ie

Agencies for Seeking Help

The Anti-Bullying Centre (ABC) – provides advice, guidance, counselling and resource materials for parents, schools, organisations and researchers: www.dcu.ie/abc

ISPCC Childline online – provides online advice and counselling service for children under eighteen: www.childline.ie

Counselling Directory – Ireland's largest independent directory of accredited counsellors/psychotherapists and counselling/psychotherapy services: www.counsellingdirectory.ie

Parentline – guides and supports parents and families: www.parentline.ie

UK and International Websites

UK
http://www.childnet.com/resources
http://www.nidirect.gov.uk

USA
http://www.cyberbullying.us

Canada
http://www.cyberbullying.org

187

Australia
http://www.cybersmart.gov.au

New Zealand
http://netsafe.org.nz

For a more comprehensive list of websites, see M. O'Moore and P. Stevens, eds, *Bullying in Irish Education: Perspectives in Research and Practice* (Cork: Cork University Press, 2013), pp. 316–19

To Report Internet Abuse
Stopcyberbullying.org/reportfbabuse